Acknowledgements

C000184319

This book and its contents would not have been possible without th

The Bakers of France, too many to list, who gave their time an
was exceptional, their enthusiasm boundless.

Special thanks to **Patric and Monique Bastiani**.

The staff of **Ecole du Boulangerie et Patisserie Paris**.

Gregory Moultry for his help with all things technical and French.

Eric Littzelmann for assistance with natural fermentation.

Recipe tester **Judy Samuels**, tasters **Dennis and Glenis Woodward**

Proof readers and grammatical support team **Lynne Hinchliff and Ruth North**

Ester North for my first baking lessons

Rod Pawsey for source materials

Darrel Moody and staff at The Sheffield City College

My wife Jenny for endless and patient support through the six years of research and travel to produce this book.

Bishop Honoré of Amiens, Patron Saint of Bakers, who gave me the inspiration for this book

Foreword

"I have a lovely image of Chris-the-Baker travelling through the French Provences in pursuit of the secrets of perfect, authentic French bread….secrets he has shared with my lucky students and with you in the pages of this book.

The journey has been a labour of love and such a worthy cause as, after all, good home-style French bread is the best thing in the world."

Julie Byrne

Principal of Sheffield City College and Executive Director

"I first met Chris in 2002, when he asked me if I could demonstrate French breads to his bakery students at The Sheffield College. We immediately appreciated each other as we shared the same passion for bread and its history. So when Chris asked me to write a foreword for his book about St. Honoré, Bakers Patron Saint and his travels through France, I had no problem in saying yes.

I found the idea of reading about his travels in all those different regions of France and the ability to bake the original breads from those same regions fantastic, it is like a taste of history in our own homes."

Gregory Moutry

Moul-bie Commercial Director United Kingdom and Scandinavia

First published in 2015 by Challenge Publications
Copyright © Christopher H.J. North 2015

Challenge Publications,
7 Earlsmere Drive, Ardsley, Barnsley S71 5HH.
www.chall-pub.co.uk

ISBN 978-1-903568-75-0

Section One

An Introduction to Bread Making

Bread in some form or other will be eaten by people as far south as *Capo de Hornos* (Cape Horn). Due north from there bread of some type is eaten all the way to Tibet. They are partial to barley bread in Tibetan homes. They bake it daily, amongst the prayer flags that wave beneath the roof of the world. Bread for most people will be made from wheat, rye, barley or whatever grows near by. The type of cereal that they have will influence the finished bread. Wheat and rye contain gluten, a type of protein at varying amounts. Leven bread requires gluten levels between 9% and 13% to make bread successfully. The ideal amount is 11% to 12%. Flat bread can be made with lower levels of gluten. The gluten quantity and quality will influence the final volume and shape of the bread. Oats, maize and barley contain little or no gluten. Bread made from these tend to be cooked on a griddle e.g. oats cakes or buck wheat for blinis, crêpes and galette.

My first introduction to the pleasure of making bread was with my Grandmother in Wakefield, West Yorkshire. On my visits to the family home, I would watch her produce oven bottom breads (a bread like fougasse without the cuts) in a Yorkshire range. This oven/cooker provided the family home with heat for baking and cooking. It was coke fired and had very little in the way of controls, no thermostat, just more or less coke and wood. Suitability for baking was decided by how a splash of water spluttered and spat on the oven sole.

I loved baking bread, and on my fortnightly visits would help with the weekend baking session and always ate more than my share. As a youth I started work in my friend's father's bakery before going off to college and working in industry. I have been fortunate enough to spend time in bakeries in Spain, France, Germany, Holland, Malta and the USA. The principal that binds them all together is a need to produce good bread.

A brief history of bread making

I have read many accounts of how bread might have first been produced; this then is a baker's view of how it could have happened.

For thousands of years the people of the Western Hemisphere followed migrating animals. These people travelled north in summer as the herds of deer and other migrating animals moved to the best grazing. In winter they turned south with these animals, they carried but few possessions, so little is known about these people or their lives.

Slowly, over thousands of years, these tribes evolved into hunter gatherers, building their homes on the high ground and protecting themselves from wild animals by building walls of thorn branches. Family groups formed for mutual support, with hunters ranging out of the settlements and gatherers finding anything seasonal available to eat. Roots, berries and grains would be available to these people to supplement their diet. Grains contain starch and the best way to access this starch is to crush and damage the grains protective coating. We know the people of these tribes made clay pots to cook in and grave excavations have provided evidence of charred grains in clay beakers.

The ancient hunter gatherers picked grains, to cook in clay pots. These grains would form a sort of porridge when heated. Should the pot fall and spill some of its contents into the fire, the results would be something similar to an oatcake (known in the industry as a "happy accident"). As a Boy Scout, we cooked on an open fire and if our sausages fell into the fire, we would recover them. I think the ancients would have done the same, or gone hungry!

There would be little or no change until the Romans paddled across the Channel. Rome brought soldiers and administrators to help in the task of expanding the empire. They needed their daily bread, and Rome had its millers and bakers, who travelled with the Legions bringing portable millstones. The Romans introduced and built the first ovens in Britain, The oven would not fully replace the bake stone or griddle but many locals are thought to have adopted the Roman way of life.

Spelt was the grain used by the Romans for their daily bread, mixed with honey, salt and water it could be produced easily and was a large part of a soldier's rations. So it was, in Britannica, until the legions were withdrawn to protect Rome from the barbarians and anyone with a grudge against the failing Empire. For many the Roman way of life continued, for most it was much as before with bread baked on hot stones or porridge as a staple diet.

More new technology came to Britain (after several invasions from Scandinavia) courtesy of the Norman French. Much like the Romans they too had soldiers and administrators who needed feeding. They brought many changes in food styles, herbs and yeast raised bread, cider and garlic. They like the Romans were brutal in their approach to the local population, so I suspect the average man in the street was just grateful to get by. People made bread out of any grains they could get their hands on, barley, rye, early forms of wheat and dried peas and beans all would be used. If you are hungry who cares what the grains are as long as they fill you up!

Up at the chateau, flour was sieved through muslin and even silk for the King and his nobles, but for Joe Public there was no change. By the 15th century rye was grown for bread. In good years it was possible to get two crops, it grew on poor ground and appeared to be fairly hardy, in fact ideal for bread. However in the 1600s there are thought to have been many poor harvests. Wet summers and damp rye crops produced a new threat to the people of Europe and the Colonies (see "Ergotisme, the Devil's Kiss"). As a result of Ergotisme, rye was rejected over a fairly brief period of time in much of England. Experimentation with oats, barley and dried peas and beans led to wheat being adopted for bread making. The Scots could only grow oats successfully at that time, so perhaps they had no reason to change their staple grain.

France and Europe had their problems with rye and Ergotisme, but appeared not to have made the break with rye as a grain for bread making. Prior to the revolution bread in France became adulterated with all sorts of poor quality grains and seeds. As the excessive taxes levied on the people brought the population to its knees, the struggle to survive began. Bad harvests in 1787 and 1788 and a recession had sparked riots in Rennes, Orleans, Lyon and further south in Aix-en Provence and Marseilles. Food shops and grain stores were looted in order to access vital food. The home of a famous wallpaper manufacturer called Reveillon was attacked because it was rumoured that he had said a worker could live on 15 sous a day, when a 2kg loaf of bread alone cost 8 sous.

On the 5th of October 1789, the Parisian people were further angered that the King had sent troops to Paris, rather than bread. A crowd of women 6,000 strong, armed with pikes and scythes marched on Versailles. Milling around the palace gates the crowd demanded bread. They shouted for the "baker" and the "baker's wife" – the King and Queen. Early next day, October 6th, the angry, hungry mob found a side gate open and flooded into the palace. A large group of mainly women set off to search the palace for the Queen. Finding her apartments, they screamed "we will make lace out of your entrails if we find you". The Queen made a hasty exit from her bedrooms, via a passageway to the King's apartments. Avoiding the mob for a few moments, they became trapped in one of the state rooms. With the mob baying for blood, a detachment of Lafayette's National Guard tried desperately to stop the women carrying out their threat.

Brioche à tête

The royal family were eventually escorted to Paris and placed in the Tuileries Palace, to await their fate. "We will not lack for bread in the future" they told the waiting crowds. "We are bringing you the baker and the baker's wife" The guillotine, "a cool breath on the back of the neck" said Dr Joseph-Ignace Guillotine. January 21st 1793 "citizen Louis Capet" was guillotined, "I die innocent" the King said calmly from the scaffold. On October 16th the Queen, Marie Antoinette age 37, joined her husband.

To be fair to the bakers and millers, they had been caught in the middle of one of France's worst depressions. The price of everything had gone sky high; people could no longer pay the high cost of flour. Consequently the millers used anything that came to hand to cheapen the grist. The colour of the bread was poor having a greyish look and so they sought to improve the colour with the addition of chemicals and ground animal bones.

After the Revolution and its excesses, the new French Government introduced purity regulations to govern just what could be put into bread. Flour, salt, yeast and water, only these ingredients could be used, the flour could be wheat or rye. Addition of oats, barley and approved seeds could be legally mixed into the dough. No fat, butter, sugar or eggs were permitted in bread, this could be used for brioche, but citizens didn't eat brioche did they?

English and French baking appears to have gone their separate ways on or around the time of the industrial revolution. Up to that point the French oven baked breads were similar to English loaves. Then with the advent of railways, steel and tin from Cornwall it began to change. The UK moved into proving and baking in tins for convenience. As more people left the land and worked in factories, less bread was produced in the home. Large bakeries filled the need for bread in large industrial towns and cities, automation of sorts followed. In France the village system was to have an oven for everyone's use; for most people bread would be made locally for many more years.

New milling techniques allowed the starch, bran and germ to be separated. White bread, once the food of the rich, was available to the poor. However, the poor got the worst deal, as bleached white flour made bread was lacking much of the natural goodness. Amazingly, the rich took to eating wholemeal for its natural benefits. Bread was still fermented for hours and had some flavour and texture about it. Then about the time I entered the industry, there came the Chorleywood bread making process. With the aid of a machine that could mix dough in three minutes, some chemicals and extra water, bread could be made. Dough was shaped after ten minutes, raised up in thirty to forty minutes and baked in a similar time. Bread was often baked with steam in order to maximise profit and avoid a lot of crumb loss when it was sliced and then bagged.

The vast majority of people lost the joy of eating real bread, even forgot how to use a bread knife. Mass produced breads are not uncommon in France, in-store bakeries are perhaps the biggest threat to small artisan bakers. The difference is fat and chemicals. In the United Kingdom bread contains fat and emulsifiers, to name but a few. Because of the old traditional purity regulations, French bread has none of these. This requires bread to be baked every day and most bakers bake three times each day or continuously. So UK bread is a day old before you get it and with fat and chemicals like mould inhibitors it will last for four to five days. The French buy it often in smaller amounts and so they have a shorter supply chain, so they buy local. You can even get bread from a slot machine in France if you miss the baker's closing time.

This book takes us back to our panary roots, all the things we lost through automation and

industries need to make greater profit. You can retrace your ancestor's foot steps and produce real bread again. We still have some excellent bakers in the UK but town planning put yellow lines outside their bakeries helping to close them down. Other shops pretend to make the bread on the premises and fool the public into thinking it's made locally. It is delivered in the night to the shop by a big truck, which comes direct from the factory. In-store bakers open boxes of frozen artisan breads, again from a factory. These are baked in store, for your convenience or is it theirs?

Perhaps now is the time to give your taste buds a thrill. Explore this book, wander through its pages and prepare to taste real bread again.

My book has everything you will need to get you started with your first bread. It continues with traditional and modern mixing methods, including various ways of fermenting your doughs. It contains recipes from the simple to the more complex, so you will have confidence to produce breads for any meal or occasion.

You will be able to produce breads with seeds and grains, fish, cheese, meat, fruits and nuts. Forty classical and new recipes are linked to forty places in France. All of these locations have some interesting historical and modern information included in these pages. The first part of the book includes a children's section, while information on folklore and myth can be found in section three. There are also guides to aid you in choosing the right type of bread to serve with various classical French meals.

Some books you buy as a gift. This is the one you keep for yourself, or buy two!

Saint Honoré and the Recipe Book

On my first visit to the *Ecole de Boulangerie et Pâtisserie de Paris*, (I will refer to it as the Paris Bakery School in future) I had arrived early for my fact finding visit. I had an appointment to meet with Thierry, the school's coordinator. Nursing my cup of coffee, I noticed a carved wooden statue of a Bishop in an adjacent display cabinet. After our initial meeting I asked Thierry about the statue and he told me that this was an image of Saint Honoré, the patron saint of bakers, confectioners and pastry chefs. I knew the name, having made pâtisserie items that bore his name. The seeds of curiosity had been sown, but they lay dormant for some years.

Retirement, forced on me by ill health, was an opportunity to find time to visit France and find some of these recipes or at least the principles that governed them. Enter Bishop Honoré of Amiens, the evangelising, travelling Bishop who was the chosen patron of bakers. Honoré's travels would be my template but there was no record of where he went. Fortunately, the Pilgrim's routes are well known and documented and so I could use them.

Statue of Saint Honoré in Amiens

One evening I was listening to the radio, the subject was authors and how they had written their books. One of the members of this discussion group said, "a book is a beginning, an end and a muddle." I liked that and how true.

My wife Jenny and I set sail for France armed with a laptop, a new camera, note pads, reference books and lots of enthusiasm. The plan was to find and travel some of the pilgrim routes and see what we could find. The first year of our travels was like a trolley dash; I took photographs and collected recipes and ideas. At night I recorded my findings on the laptop. The material was unrelated and could only serve as a reference point for where we had been; a sort of diary account.

Year two was a little more structured and we travelled further south. Our route took us towards Spain and the eventual end of the Pilgrim's journey. Jenny and I filled in extra places of interest as we travelled around the country.

Our third year as pilgrims found us with a structured approach and a plan for the middle (no longer a muddle) and we were able to target places to visit. The Michelin map had coloured spots to indicate our visits and the Michelin Guide to France served to point me to places I had not considered. The French Tourist Board representatives have been most helpful as we have investigated more and more places of interest.

By now the structure of the recipes had changed. Originally, I had intended the book to be a reference for bakery students. The recipes were first intended for production in colleges and industry. Now the recipes are scaled down to suit the home baker but it can still be a useful recipe book for Artisanal work in college or industry.

Year four was one of reflection, as some areas, like the pain biologic and the pain traditional that used exclusively Levain naturel, had not been fully explored. The number of recipes I had gathered had exceeded sixty but I felt that I had to stop. In order to make the recipes representative of as many styles and recipe contents, I stopped at forty.

I have met with shop assistants, bakery workers, artisans, millionaires and even a Marquis; they have all helped in the production of this book of French breads. I am grateful to everyone who has taken and used their valuable time to answer my questions and provide me with vital information and has allowed me to work in their bakery.

The information about the towns and places we have visited do not always line up with Bishop Honoré's travel dates. Châteaux Pimpean and Brissac had not been built. Honoré might have visited Avignon as it was a cultural and religious centre, but the Popes did not move there until the early 14th Century. All that said, the history and anecdotal remarks are intended to add a little flavour of the place. It might even serve as the basis of some after dinner conversation. The book has been written to inform, educate and amuse. I apologise in advance for any historical inaccuracies.

I do hope you will go on to make some wonderful French bread in your home. You have in this book forty recipes; some are classical, regional and in some cases my idea of suitable formulation for person or place. The recipes have been selected to be suitable for most tastes and occasions. Recipes in this book include ones with meat, fish, cheese, fruit, herbs, nuts and seeds. The extra ingredients like cheese or seeds can be changed, increased in quantity or omitted, it's your choice. The methods of mixing range from simple to complex, mixing methods being inter-changeable.

I would like to thank my family and friends, for without them, this book would be little more than a pile of unrelated papers and recipes. Lastly thanks to my wife Jenny; Sherpa, driver, critic and supporter, to whom I dedicate the book and the recipe Saint Genix.

Chris North.

9

Safe Working in the Kitchen

Making bread is not a dangerous occupation. However, there are many opportunities to create potential dangers. The main areas to consider are:

Electrical Equipment

Mixers should be well maintained and used to the manufacturer's specification.
Do not clean them while they are operating, unplug before cleaning.

Personal Safety

Secure long hair and loose sleeves when working with mixing machines.

Ventilation

Keep the kitchen well ventilated at all times. Oven fumes can build up in unventilated rooms. These are not good for your health.

Ovens

Hot gases and steam can burn, stand back when you open the oven door to avoid the rush of hot gases. Roll your sleeves down when getting produce out of the oven to avoid burns. Hot surfaces e.g. baking trays from the oven, use substantial, grease free, dry oven cloths.

Children

Children are fascinated by baking, it's fun, it's food and it has its dangers too.

- Floors and surfaces should be kept dry and clean to avoid slipping.

- Knives and blades - keep them in a safe place. Do not put then in the sink, a blade in soapy water can cut you but be unseen.

- Clean dough from your hands by washing, don't let it dry on your skin and then rub it off.

- Use barrier cream and gloves if you have sensitive skin.

- Flour and nuts can cause allergic reaction in some rare cases.

- It is always wise to consider your personal health first. This applies to everyone, not just children.

For those who did not work safely!

Ancillary Equipment

Baking Mats. They are expensive but if used carefully they will last for years and reduce the need to prepare the surface of baking trays. These mats will reduce fumes that come off oiled/greased trays.

Bowls or Baskets. Are good for the final proving of round bread dough. This will keep its shape as unsupported dough at this stage will flow. *NB.* Make sure you allow for the expansion of the dough.

Brushes. The type of wallpaper brush used to remove air pockets. This is useful for keeping flour under control on the work top, (called a bench brush in the industry).

Coffee grinder. Good for reducing oats and malted barley into a flour. Also, seeds like caraway and fennel can be reduced to a course powder

Cooling Wires/Trays. You will need 2 of these. They are mesh to allow the air to circulate all round the hot bread. Without these trays the bread will sweat and loose the crisp crust.

Craft Knife. This is used to cut the surface of the dough prior to baking.

Large Plastic Bowl/Container. For proving the dough, make sure there is room for the dough to expand.

Linen Tea Cloths. Good for covering the dough and also the final proving for baguettes (corrugated).

Measuring Jug. For the water, 1.5 litre size is best.

Oven Thermometer. This is very important to confirm the accuracy of your oven thermostat settings.

Plastic Bowls. One large and smaller ones to put the measured ingredients in.

Rolling Pins. Standard size and a thin one (cut from a new broom handle). Wooden tools should not be soaked in water. Clean them with a damp cloth dry naturally and store. Soaked rolling pins can end up warping like a banana.

Scales. Electric and balance.

Scissors and Scrapers are useful tools.

Small Brushes. Useful for preparing trays and applying egg or milk to the surface of the dough. Ensure they are sterilised and dried after using.

Thermometer. Alcohol type (range 0°C to 100°C) is useful for measuring water and dough temperatures. *Caution:* never use the old mercury thermometer.

Water Spray. Used to moisten dough as it proves both at pre and post baking stages.

Wooden slip. Use when placing baguettes into the oven. A 40cm length of decorative tongue and groove board (or similar) will suffice.

Tins, Trays and Their Care

There are no good light weight baking tins and trays. Non stick coatings are alright for occasional use for example on brioche tins. For regular use you need a heavy gauge tray with (if you must) a high quality non stick coating. Steel trays with silicone baking sheet/mats are best. You can replace the silicone sheet periodically.

Never use abrasive scrubbing pads on your non stick ware or cut bread through on the surface. New tins are best it they are black. Wash and grease them before using. Bread sticking can be a problem with new tins.

Solution

(a) Leave the bread to sweat a little and then knock the tin edge (upside down) to remove the bread.

(b) Use a plastic spatula to remove the bread. Prepare again with care using vegetable fat or lard, not oil.

New shining silver tins need to be "blued". To do this, place the tin/tray in a very hot oven lightly greased for 15 minutes. *NB:* Open the windows to vent the air. This process may need to be repeated a few times prior to baking.

Second hand trays/tins that are older and blackened are worth looking out for. Good quality and well used tins/trays are excellent to bake in, but not rusty tins.

You can wash non-stick ware, soak it if any sugar residue burns on. Other tins and trays should be cleaned with a paper towel or cloth while still warm. Continued baking builds up a patina, this helps the bread to be released from your tins and trays. Washing removes this patina and could cause rust to form. Using a sharp knife to remove bread will only cause the tin to stick to the bread even more.

The French, traditionally, do not use baking tins for their breads, still there are a few around and I have taken a picture to give you an idea of what to look out for.

Note: if you need to leave dough on steel trays for more than a few hours, (eg. overnight in the fridge), do make sure you use a sheet of baking parchment or a silicone baking sheet. Uncoated steel will transfer rust spots onto the base of your bread and will not improve the taste.

1 Brioche tins

4 Enamel steel tray

2 Steel tray blackened with use

5 Non-stick demi baguette

3 Loaf tin suitable for pain de mie

Recipes and How They Work

This is for your guidance. Recipes are many and varied. In France there are national recipes as well as some regional and local bakers' versions. It is normal to use the "Baker's percentage", that is the flour weight = 100%. All other ingredients are then a percentage related to the flour weight.

Flour	100%
Water	64%
Salt	1.6%
Yeast	2.0%

This percentage system allows you to see the relationship of each ingredient to the flour. If you should wish to increase or decrease any ingredients, keep a record of these changes on your recipe. Flour being the largest ingredient will affect the amount of water in any recipe.

The type and quality of the flour you choose to use will also decide the amount of water used. The higher the gluten or protein contents of the flour the greater the amount of water it will absorb and carry. Wholemeal and brown flours absorb most because bran is like blotting paper. Some English bakers do not fully understand this. This is why some wholemeal bread is harsh and dry to eat (see "Autolysis").

Weighing and Measuring Ingredients

I use metric units for my recipes. The baker's percentage works well as flour at 100% becomes, by adding a zero, 1000g or a kilo. Add a zero to any percentage and you get a basic recipe. I started out life as a baker with drams, ounces, pounds, stones, pints etc.

Electric digital scales are good for small amounts of material. For larger amounts, I would use balanced scales. Check your digital scales with a metric weight. Most digital scales allow you to zero after each ingredient is added to the bowl on the scale.

Note: yeast must not be placed with salt or sugar, keep them apart. Be accurate especially with salt and yeast.

Fluid measures

1 litre = 1kg.

Use a jug with gradients on the side.

13

Bread Making Ingredients

Flour

Bread making flours must have a protein content of 11% or more and are best if labelled extra strong. Bread flours come as wholemeal, brown and white. If you look around in the supermarkets you can find flours that contain malt flour and grains.

Specialist mills produce flours like rye and spelt and seed grain mixtures are also available in big supermarkets and specialist shops. You may also blend your own, using a bread making flour as the base, then add your own seeds. Herbs can be added to this mélange or you may add wheat germ or extra bran if you prefer.

It is worth mentioning that both oats and barley are used in multi grain/flour blends. Oats and barley contain little gluten and cannot be used to produce bread in its accepted form. Mix grains, oats and barley with high protein (strong flour) and it will make interesting and pleasant eating.

Salt

Table salt is fine to use for bread making. It is used at various rates in France, e.g. 1.8% to 2.0% or 18 to 20g per 1000g of flour. In Britain the Government has forced industry to reduce its salt additions to bread and this is on average 1.5% or 15 grams to 1000 grams of flour.

At home the choice is yours, just as it is with salt in cooking. I will just add my view, and that is that adequate fermentation and good ingredients improve flavour, reducing the need for high levels of salt in bread. Salt adds flavour and controls/slows fermentation in the dough. Sea salt contains iodine and this has the effect of further slowing fermentation. If sea salt is used, the solution is to add a little extra yeast or it will take longer to ferment.

French flour

Yeast

Dried or fresh, the choice is yours. Fresh yeast is available in most supermarkets on the chill counter. Ask the staff, as it is often hard to locate. Yeast is a sugar fungus, but a baker's yeast has been developed to have a greater tolerance to temperature changes than brewers and wine yeasts.

Yeast is everywhere - it can be seen on black grapes and plums as a grey/white bloom. The yeast is on the surface of the grape and waits only for it to ripen. As the grape ripens, the sugar content of the fruit goes up. The fruit fall and fermentation starts. This form of wild yeast is at the heart of traditional French bread making. The grapes, plums, apples or wheat are encouraged to ferment flour and water.

The important thing to remember about yeast is to treat it like a baby, too hot and you will kill it, too cold and it stops working. Ideal fermentation conditions require warmth, food and time.

Hostile ingredients to yeast are salt, sugar and acid in all but small amounts. Less than 2% of flour weight is a good guide.

Fresh yeast keeps in a fridge for up to 2 weeks, dried for a year.

As yeast feeds on sugars like maltose it also softens the protein and produces flavour and most important at the final stage CO_2. Yeast action in fermenting dough is a highly complex affair and needs to be researched if necessary in a specialist book.

Water

Water quality is not a problem in Great Britain. Hard water can inhibit fermentation a little, compensate with 0.5% yeast. It is important to measure water accurately and also ensure it is not hot or you will damage or kill the yeast.

Fats and Oils

Strictly speaking French bread does not contain fat or oil but some specialist types do. The effect of fat on bread is to soften the crust and crumb. The true French baguette will not contain fat but an English one does, this serves to extend the shelf life of the English baguette. In France bakers bake 3 times a day 7 days a week in order that the bread is fresh and at its best. Traditional fermented breads will keep a little longer than the basic baguette.

Seeds and Grains

• Pumpkin

• Millet

• Sesame

• Barley

• Oats

• Sunflower

These are examples of the many types of seeds that can be mixed in or placed on French bread, and their use is all down to personal taste. It is a good idea to consider if any of the family has seed or nut allergies prior to embarking on their use. Some seeds are best toasted if they are to be used inside the loaf but not if they are to go on top. Linseeds (both yellow and brown), are good for women's health, as they are a natural source of plant oestrogens. I like seeds in my bread but not everyone does.

Fruit and Nuts

In many regional types of bread, fruit and nuts are very popular. Hazelnuts, sweet chestnuts, pine nuts and almonds and many more are used. Fruit, mostly dried or preserved are used in combination with nuts. Figs, apricots, dates, melon and raisins are often used fresh. Soft fruits are not on the whole employed in bread dough as they bleed juices into the dough and disappear in the mixing. Raspberries, blackberries, strawberries etc. are examples of such soft fruit. NB. Remember, nuts can cause an allergic reaction for some people.

Gluten

Gluten is the protein from wheat flour and can be purchased in powder form. In France it is added to rye bread, pain complet and pain au son, to give increased volume. It is not an essential ingredient, used at 2% to the flour weight. I have not included it in my recipes. If you can source it, you can include it in your recipes.

Cornmeal

Cornmeal is made from maize and being gluten free it has to be used with wheat flour to make bread eg. pain au mais.

Buckwheat Flour

Buckwheat flour has little or no gluten and so it is not used for bread making. Buckwheat is used in France to produce crêpes and galettes.

Milk Powder

Available at most supermarkets. Milk powder contains lactose which caramelises in baking giving colour and flavour to the bread crust. Use 2% to flour weight.

Malt (dark)

Malt is a valuable yeast food, used at 0.5% (5g to 1kg of flour). Good in winter if cold conditions inhibit fermentation. Avoid light malt as it creates rapid uncontrolled fermentation and has little or no flavour.

Honey

Honey is a natural source of sweetness. It can be used in bread making but care must be taken as honey will cause breads and cakes to colour (turn brown) quickly, in the oven. Baking temperatures need to be reduced as the amount of honey used increases.

Citric Acid

Limited in France to rye bread or rye and wheat breads, this counters the natural tendency for rye bread doughs to become sticky. This aids handling and I find 1% to flour weight works.

Wine Vinegar

This is added to rye bread at 1% to 2% to flour weight this will aide volume and stability. Pre-ferment dough, see mixing section.

Rice Flour and Semolina (coarse ground)

These are used under dough to aid movement on surfaces, and can also be used for dusting and decoration of bread.

Eggs (hens)

Eggs will be used in products like brioche. They enrich, soften, flavour and colour baked products. An egg will moisten its own weight of flour and will extend the shelf life of most baked products. Egg is used as a glaze with equal amounts of milk. Always store eggs in a fridge and remember they could be a source of salmonella bacteria.

Bread wheat

Mixing Methods

All or most of the dough ingredients are placed in a bowl and mixed together with water. This distributes the ingredients, moistens the flour and evens out the temperature and then forms the dough. Mixing continues for approximately 15 minutes with any adjustments to the water being made at this stage.

This extra mixing will fully develop a matrix of protein strands, giving a smooth stretchy mixture. If it is not smooth and stretchy, the water content is reviewed: is it wet enough? If not, more water is added and the dough is mixed for a further 5 minutes (I do not think you can over mix dough by hand but it is possible to over mix dough by machine. Over mixed dough is rare; it will be warmer and stickier than planned).

The successfully mixed dough is then covered and placed in a warm area to ferment. How long this takes depends on how the yeast is used and how warm the dough is maintained.

A rough guide is 1% yeast at 24°C will take 3 hours, 2% = 2 hours and 3% yeast will ferment in 1 hour. Salt levels, fat, sugar, spice and eggs will slow fermentation down (see "Fermentation").

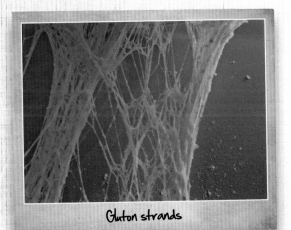
Gluten strands

Methode Directe (straight dough)

This is perhaps the simplest method to start with. All the ingredients are placed in the mixing bowl, and then water with its temperature adjusted to suit the dough temperature is added. Mixing by hand takes about 20 minutes to achieve smooth and stretchy dough.

Methode Directe (straight dough, French artisan)

Hold back a small amount of water and the salt and proceed as above. Mix for all but the last 5 minutes, then add the salt softened in a small amount of water and continue mixing until all the salt is taken up by the dough.

This method encourages protein (gluten) development and helps the dough to take up more water without being over sticky. The French view more water in the dough gives improved bread.

Levain-Levure (sponge and dough)

This is a two-stage mixing. First between 25% and 50% of the flour is placed in a bowl and all the water and the yeast is added. These ingredients are mixed together for 5 minutes, then left to stand and ferment. This gives the yeast an ideal environment to reproduce, which will in turn give an improved flavour and the texture to the bread.

This produces a "sponge" which is then added to the remaining ingredients and mixed as in the straight dough method. The method is traditionally used for fermentation periods of over an hour's duration.

Ferment and Dough

This English method works well with viennoiseries such as brioche. Again, this is a two-stage mixing method, used more for speed than flavour, it encourages rapid fermentation. This method is used before ingredients such as spices, egg, sugar and fat, which inhibit fermentation, are added to the dough.
In short, the yeast is given a head start before the materials that hold back fermentation are added.

The ferment consists of 10% of the flour by weight, the yeast and water at 38°C stirred together, covered and set aside in a warm place for 20 minutes. Lumps in the ferment will disperse in mixing. A good ferment should have a slight convex curve to its surface and have little explosions of gas breaking through it. On close inspection it looks like the surface of the moon, with tiny craters. The ferment is then added to the rest of the ingredients and mixed as in method directe.

Poolish (liquid sponge)

Another two-stage mix - a softer version of the sponge and dough method. About 20% of the flour, water and yeast are roughly mixed together and set aside to ferment. There are many recipes used for sponges and the ratio of flour to water varies as does the yeast quantity. The intention in all sponge recipes is to create an ideal environment for the yeast to reproduce. Yeast needs a liquid, warm place with access to food source and time. Given these conditions you will stimulate fermentation and with it comes all the benefits of good dough condition and flavour.

Pate Fermentee (pre-fermented dough)

A common method of mixing in France that uses approximately 30% of either left over dough or some made in advance for the specific purpose. The dough remaining after you have mixed can be reserved for your next bread mix, e.g. 300 grams put into a sealed container or a plastic bag and placed in the fridge. Remove it from the fridge the night before, use and add it to your next bread mix.

You can add white pre-fermented dough to rye bread but you should increase the rye flour to the white recipe to keep the ratios correct. For wholemeal and brown it is best to keep the pre-fermented dough specifically brown or wholemeal. This basically is methode directe with the added pre-ferment mixed in. Add this at the mid point of the mixing time to avoid excessive oxidation.

Autolysis - *Discovered by Raymond Calvel*

First the flour and water in the recipe are mixed together slowly for 3 to 4 minutes then rested for 13 minutes. After the remaining ingredients are added, the dough is then mixed for a further 8 minutes. If the recipe has 1% yeast and 2% salt, the approximate first fermentation time will be 4 to 6 hours at 24 centigrade. Scale the dough into unit's weight. Rest for 30 minutes then mould and shape the dough.

The second fermentation is 90 minutes, after which it is baked. This method can be used with most recipes.

Mixing and Mixing Machines

Hand Mixing

You can mix perfectly well by hand, it is therapeutic, tones the upper body and if you are angry for any reason, it is a great way to work it off. Bread dough takes about twenty minutes to fully mix and develop and can be done by the whole family.

Dough must be extensible, smooth and as moist as you can cope with, remember dry dough makes dry bread. Your first 5 minutes is spent mixing the ingredients together and forming the dough. The remaining 15 minutes is spent developing the protein structure and making it stretchy, and extensible. Think for a moment about bubble gum, in order to produce a good sized bubble, you must first warm, moisten and chew the gum. Nothing will happen in the case of the gum if this process is not followed.

Bread mixing aims to achieve something similar. Warm water moistens the protein (gluten), mixing is a little like chewing and the yeast produces CO_2 gas to blow thousands of little bubbles in the structure.

Mixing Machines

Mixing bread by machine might be necessary due to the sheer physical input required. Here is some advice to consider if you plan to make a purchase:

- Mixing bread requires a lot of work on the part of the machine and overloading it will cause the motor to burn out quickly. Choose a semi-professional machine with the biggest electrical motor in the range.

- Choose a stainless steel bowl (two bowls would be useful) and mix on low/medium speed to protect your machine from overload.

- Never mix dough with a cake attachment (K beater) or on fast speed, it is dangerous and will damage your machine. Larger domestic machines will mix 1kg of flour into the bread dough, however if you find that your mixer is struggling to cope, take half the mixture out.

- Always use a hook attachment for bread dough and don't be tempted to clear the inside of the bowl with your fingers or a tool while the mixer is in motion.

Speciality Breads

You can be creative because bread dough is, if you wish, a blank canvas with which you can experiment. Make a note of any additions and review and record the results. There is nothing more annoying than creating a perfect combination and not being able to recall the amount of olives to bacon!

Herbs can lessen in strength due to age and the time of the year they are harvested and from where they came.

Note: These amounts are only a guide, based on 1kg of flour.

Cumin bread	18g ground cumin seeds
Thyme bread	12g thyme finely chopped
Garlic bread	85g garlic peeled and chopped
Onion bread	500g onion chopped and browned over a low heat,(use just warm)
Fennel bread.	14g ground fennel seeds. This is nice to serve with fish
Poppy seed bread	130g poppy seeds, lightly toasted
Cheese bread	160g strong flavoured cheese chilled and cubed.
Parmesan bread	145g parmesan cheese, split into 85g and 60g - grate 85g into the dough, cube 60g to use as decoration on the loaves.
Seaweed or Algae bread	90g of powdered algae/seaweed, might need to be pre-soaked before use.
Bacon bread	135g of diced smoked bacon, sauté and cool. Add at the end of mixing cycle
Toulouse sausage bread	260g Toulouse sausage, cooked and sliced. Add at the end of mixing cycle.
Olive bread	130g pitted green and black olives, finely chopped and air dried prior to use. Olives should be added with care at the end of the mixing cycle

Have lots of fun, the only thing that will restrict you is your imagination. Other herbs can be substituted for the ones on the list, my advice is to start low and increase amounts of herbs or other ingredients until you have it to your individual taste.

Dark rye bread

French bread selection

Yeast Quantities, Temperature and Fermentation

The fault with much of our modern bread is that it has been rushed. Mixing methods, chemicals, higher quantities of yeast and maximum proving temperatures will produce a loaf. The loaf will have good texture for sandwiches but it will lack that all important flavour. Conversely, small, even minute quantities of yeast, will give the dough that important long fermentation time. Cooler doughs in storage will allow fermentation periods of 12 to 18 hours i.e. the made up dough is stored overnight at 5°C. Many of us will not want the kitchen tied up for days, if so, a 3 hour poolish could be a better choice.

There are materials and conditions that will inhibit yeast fermentation; salt, high levels of fat, eggs and sugar are some of them, and our traditional hot cross bun is a good example of a yeast inhibitor. It is sometimes necessary to compensate for yeast inhibitors by the choice of mixing method, e.g. by using ferments and poolishes or by adding an extra 1% of yeast.

At home the rate of fermentation is not normally critical, however in industry timing is important. Ingredient temperatures and ambient temperatures will vary through the seasons. Water temperature in the dough can be used to compensate, for example in high summer ambient temperatures you can use cold water, mid–winter warmer water.

The formula used is 2 x dough temperature, minus the flour temperature = the water temperature, so check the dough temperature say 22°C x 2 = 44°C minus the flour temperature 20°C = 24°C for the water. A food thermometer can be used to record the flour and then the water temperature. If you do not have a thermometer to hand just work on the baby bath temperature principal, as hot water will distress yeast or kill it. Cooler temperatures are always the safe option. Cold conditions stop fermentation (below 4°C) this is called retarding the dough.

Bread doughs can be kept retarded for 24 hours. Cover and it must not be placed on an uncoated metal tray or tin (rust spots). Enriched doughs for example, butter, eggs and sugar can be kept retarded for 2 days. Allowed to warm up gradually they will start to prove up and then can be baked as normal.

Active yeast fermentation

Levain Naturel

Levain naturel is also known as sour dough or the mother dough.

There are wild yeasts everywhere - they travel on the wind and wait for a chance to colonise some form of food. They need moisture, warmth, food and time to multiply. They have been utilised and discouraged in equal measure. Employed for beer, wine and bread making, they are an asset but also a hindrance. Thousands of tonnes of fruits are lost each year to spoilage caused by wild yeast.

Sugar in increased amounts will prevent fruit spoilage (as in jam). High levels of sugar in dough will slow and stop fermentation. Wild yeasts can be best observed on the skins of black plums and grapes; this bloom of yeasts will kick start your levain naturel. In Normandy they use apples to start the process.

Wholemeal flour is often used and rye flour can be substituted if you wish. The formula is still wild yeast, food (starch or sugar), warmth, moisture and time = fermentation. Inhibitors to this process are high levels of salt, sugar or temperature, all of which will slow or stop fermentation. I understand that once a levain naturel is established it could last a working baker's life time, so this has to be treated with care.

Levain naturel needs to be refreshed with a fresh source of food (starch/maltose) in order to keep the yeasts active. The levain must be kept scrupulously clean, no old dough put with it. The levain must not be contaminated with commercial yeast as this would become dominant over time. So make sure your bowl or machine attachments do not have any dough with bakers yeast stuck on them.

A portion of levain remaining is placed with an equal weight of flour and water. Mix lightly to form dough and put into a food grade container with a lid. *NB*: needs expansion room. If you plan to use it the next day, keep it at room temperature, it not, reserve in the refrigerator. If having a break, bag it and place in the freezer. This levain will need some TLC to get back to operational strength, it will require refreshing and holding at room temperature for a couple of days.

Purists will use only levain to ferment their doughs; other artisans will use less levain and a little baker's yeast. One baker I know uses 80% levain and one gram of bakers yeast in his 12 hour overnight dough. He does this just to reassure his bakers that it will work. It all comes down to your choice after all.

It is most important to keep your levain free from any form of contamination. The same principle applies to production of pain biologic; this must not be mixed with non accredited materials. Even the levain should be made from flour produced on naturally fertilised ground.

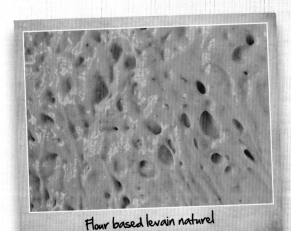

Flour based levain naturel

Sour Dough

Ingredients

Stage 1

170g	Wholemeal flour
120g	Water (38°C)

Total 290g

Stage 2

350g	Wholemeal flour
240g	Water (38°C)
290g	Stage 1 dough

Total 880g

Stage 3

560g	White bread flour
315g	Water (38°C)
880g	Stage 2 dough

Total 1.755kg

Stage 4

125g	White bread flour
630g	Water (38°C)
1.755kg	Stage 3 dough

Total 3.51kg

Stage 5

1.125kg	White bread flour
630g	Water (38°C)
3.51kg	Stage 4 dough

Total 5.265kg

Mixing method

Day 1

- Make up into a dough, place in a food grade plastic container for 24 hours at 25°C.

Day 2

- Repeat the above, using the stage 2 ingredients.

Day 3

- Repeat the above, using the stage 3 ingredients.

Day 4

- Repeat the above, using the stage 4 ingredients.
- Remove 1.755kg of dough. Reserve in a plastic bag and store in your fridge. It will keep for up to 1 week.

Stage 5 is added to bread doughs in various amounts and there are a great many recipes that can be used. As a guide, the greater the amount of levain that is used the smaller quantity of yeast. Levain quantities vary between 30% of the flour weight and up to 80% e.g. 800g of levain to 1kg of flour weight in the recipe.

A small amount of bakers yeast (levure) will also be used. The yeast quantity increases as the levain weight decreases in the recipe. The yeast will increase up to maximum of 25g per 1kg of flour in the recipe.

When yeast and sour dough are used together it is known as the *Levain Levure* method.

Chris' Not-So-Sour Dough

Ingredients

Stage 1

170g	Wholemeal flour
150g	Water (38°C)
5g	Honey
40g	Plum tops (x6)

Total 365g

Stage 2

350g	White bread flour
300g	Water
365g	Stage 1 mixture

Total 1.15kg

Stage 3

650g	White bread flour
315g	Water
50g	Natural yoghurt
1kg 15g	Stage 2 mixture

Total 1.44kg

Stage 4 - Refreshing

1.125kg	White bread flour
650g	Water (38°C)
700g	Half of stage 3 mixture

Total 2.475kg

Note: Do not add anything else to the levain e.g. commercial yeast or preferment dough. If, in your judgement, the levain does not smell or appear right, get rid of it and start again.

This can be repeated for the rest of your life. Put it in the freezer if you are going on holiday, giving it 48 hours to recover.

Mixing method

Stage 1

- Place the unwashed plum tops, minus the stalks, (the plums should show signs of yeast bloom) or 12 black grapes if plums are not available, with tepid water and 5g of honey in a bowl.
- Soak overnight or liquidise and strain.
- Mix into the flour, place into a food grade plastic bucket, (look for the wine glass sign for food grade), or suitable sized bowl for expansion.
- Cover and stand for 24 hours.

Stage 2

- Place the flour and water and stage 1 in a suitable sized bowl (expansion room).
- Cover and leave for 24 hours.

Stage 3

- Method as stage 2 plus yoghurt, leave covered for 24 hours. After 24 hours use approximately half of the mixture for baking. You can add the levain at between 30% and 80% of the flour weight of the bread recipe you are using. (See also mixing methods).
- Place the balance into a food grade container and cover, place in the fridge for the next baking session.

Stage 4

- Prior to your next baking day, take out the levain.
- Refresh the levain with stage 4 and mix together and cover for 24 hours at room temperature.
- Use approximately half to the bake with the remaining half placed back in the fridge and covered.
- Hygiene is paramount. Keep the sides of the container clean do not allow a build up of dry crusty material.
- If you are planning a large baking session, double or treble the quantity at refreshing stage.
- If it appears dry, add some extra water.

Starter Recipes

Brioche Enriched Poolish

Ingredients

125g	Strong white flour
2g	Yeast fresh
75g	Milk or water (38°C)

Total 202g

Mixing method

- Mix the yeast, milk/water and flour in a bowl.
- Cover and set aside in an ambient room temperature for 4 hours.
- Suitable for enriched dough e.g. brioche.

Basic Poolish

Ingredients

250g	Strong white flour
250g	Water (38°C)
3g	Yeast fresh

Total 503g

Mixing method

- Disperse the yeast in the water.
- Mix in the flour (a few lumps in the mixture is OK).
- Cover and stand for 3 hours.

Pre-fermented Dough

Ingredients

500g	Strong white flour
320g	Water (38°C)
6g	Salt
2g	Yeast fresh

Total 828g

Mixing method

- Mix all the ingredients together and form dough, 3 - 4 minutes only.
- Ferment in a covered container for 4 hours.
- Use or store in the fridge, ideally to be used within 3 days.

Note: always add pre-fermented doughs at the half mixed stage to avoid over mixing the final dough.

First Fermentation

This stage in the bread making process is known as bulk fermentation in the United Kingdom. First rising appears to be a term used in the United States of America. In France the first fermentation is *le pointage*. I am sure there will be others too.

At the mixing stage yeast cells are introduced into the dough. They can come from bakers yeast, fresh or dried, or via ferments. Ferments are nurseries for yeasts to multiply in, warm, fluid and with plenty of available food (maltose).

Yeast can also be added via sour dough or levain. The way yeast is added and the amount will influence the speed of fermentation. Fast fermentation is achieved by adding up to 3% yeast to flour weight to a warm dough. In commercial bakeries they use lots of additives to speed up and stabilise the dough prior to baking. This is not a method of bread making I would recommend unless you are desperate.

Yeast multiplies by a process called budding. Cells divide and increase in a dough, provided it is not too cool. Yeast can source its own food by converting starch into sugar; there is often naturally occurring maltose sugar in flour to start feeding the infant colony of yeasts. Bakers yeast is bred specifically for bread making and will tend to ferment faster than the naturally occurring yeasts of the levain naturel.

The amount of yeast needed for long fermentation periods i.e. up to 12 hours normally, is very small. The active ingredient in an aspirin is tiny, to pick it up by hand would be difficult, and to make handling practical it is placed with filler and made into a tablet. The addition of a levain to dough is similar, only a small amount of yeast is added, this avoids rapid fermentation.

Fermentation is a process of complex physical and chemical changes and there are some excellent detailed papers written on that subject. See "The Taste of Bread" by Raymond Calvel to name but one.

After 2 hours

Fermentation, in layman's terms, is the natural maturing or ripening of the dough. If dough is under-ripe it will be difficult to roll out or shape and it will make a squeaking noise when you mould it. It will tear in the last expansion in the oven, as the protein in the dough will not be sufficiently elastic, this elasticity being brought about by enzymes from the yeast softening the protein (gluten). The artisan bakers in England would liken the fermentation to the maturing of an apple. Under fermented is like a green apple, but the correct length of fermentation gives a ripe dough. Over fermentation, being spent dough, is like over ripe fruit; it will collapse and is only to be used as a pre-fermented addition to the next dough. Correctly fermented dough achieved by long fermentation has plenty of tolerance. That is to say you can give or take half an hour before it needs to be processed. Fast fermentation processes are not tolerant as these will be spoiled if taken half an hour too early or late.

Dough that is correctly fermented will be easily shaped and rolled out into baguettes. Under fermented dough will resist rolling out and keep springing back to its original shape. Under fermentation will give you bread, but it will stale rapidly and be unpleasant to eat. Over fermented dough will be soft, sticky and will not hold the shape correctly having lost all of its natural spring and structure.

Ready for de-gassing

Like an over ripe fruit it will just collapse and flow outwards and, even if you persevere with the dough, it will give you poor results. Baguettes will be flat on top not the traditional bold shaped ones we see. The inside will compact and yet will lack structure. The bread dough will flow outwards giving poor volume and appearance. The container you use for this fermentation needs to be of sufficient size to allow for expansion, must be of a food grade plastic or stainless steel and have some form of a cover. The place you keep the container and fermenting dough will also influence the speed of fermentation. A cool kitchen area will take a good deal longer than the airing cupboard or near the central heating boiler.

I am not going to tell you that in a domestic setting you can set your watch by the time the dough will be fully fermented and ready to be scaled and moulded. Experience and consistency is the key, e.g. if your recipe and dough temperature is constant and the background temperature in which the fermenting dough is held is also constant, then the dough should be ready at the same time each baking day, in fact you will be able to plan your day around it!

An ancient Tythe Barn

The Yield

This is a term for the number of units or loaves you can get out of a given recipe. The truth is that the total at the bottom of the recipe and the actual amount will vary. We lose dough on equipment and our hands. Some flours will not take up the full amount of water, reducing the total weight of dough. Conversely, if the flour weight is a little heavy then extra water may be added to get the consistency correct. This will add extra finished dough weight to the recipe.

Bread recipes, unlike those used for cakes, are fairly tolerant. An accountant will tell you that 10kg of dough on the recipe will give you 20 x 500g loaves. In fact you will get 19½ more often than not. If you need 20 loaves, pinch a little of the 19 to get 20. We at home are not governed by laws on weight.

If you have spare dough, it can be added to the next dough you are making. White will go into brown but not the other way around because it will look odd. Either white or brown will go into rye bread, or just into a polythene bag with an ID sticker and the date. You can keep it in the fridge for up to a week or it can be frozen. Provided it is clean there is no need to discard any dough In fact pre-ferment dough is a great source of flavour and enzyme energy for the next bread mix.

Lastly, little children love little loaves of bread, they cannot get enough of them. So make a mini-plait or loaf for the children, one each to avoid disappointment!

Scaling (Cutting dough to a given weight)

Bread produced in France is sold in units of weight like a baguette but can be purchased as a tranche (big slice) from a much larger loaf. Typically, large loaves baked with fruit and nuts will be sold this way on market stalls.

At home, bread for your own use (not for sale) can be scaled at any weight you like. It would be impossible to produce any of the large loaves made by craft bakers in France. A domestic oven could not accommodate 5kg of dough moulded and shaped, so we have to stay within the limits of our oven. I have produced a guide of loaf sizes and weights suitable for a domestic oven. This should assist you in the size and shape of any bread you plan to make.

It is important to try and keep bread weights constant. As for having small and large units of bread on the same tray, this will cause baking problems. The smaller rolls will be ready long before the larger units which will be unbaked.

It is best to cut dough for scaling, as tearing it damages the dough structure. A blunt knife or a plastic scraper will be ideal.

Scales can be of the balance type or electric. If you are buying new I would recommend electric, as they are more flexible.

Resting Dough

There are a number of reasons why doughs are rested between mixing stages and before moulding or shaping. Flour suitable for bread making must contain protein (gluten) so that the dough can be successfully expanded by the carbon dioxide (CO_2) produced by the yeast. Protein development is best achieved when the protein is fully hydrolysed (or wet). Incomplete or partial hydrolysing will cause the dough to be short and easily torn. Think of bubble gum: a well chewed, moist gum (sorry!) makes the best bubbles.

Bran is another ingredient that takes time to fully soak up the water in the recipe. Bran is a slow version of blotting paper.

When protein has been formed it has a memory. Just after mixing the dough will be tight and a little stiff. Mixing winds the protein up like an old clock spring. After a few minutes the protein starts to relax and forgets its previous shape. If you try to shape the dough without resting, it will tear and split.

When mixing dough for French bread, it should be as wet as possible. Not only does a fully hydrated dough give you a better shaped loaf, it will also keep longer and, in commercial baking, you get far more dough from your flour. This is one of the few cases were watering down a dough will give you a better product.

Le fournil du château

How to Shape and Mould Bread Dough

(See also the DVD included with this book)

There are some French breads that don't require moulding, e.g. *pavé*, which are just cut to approximately the right size, proved and baked. Most bread dough is cut to weight and moulded, rested and then given a shape. It is at this point perhaps worth repeating this fact. Bread dough has a short term memory so if you shape it into a ball and then try to roll it into a square, it will resist you. If you wait for 10 minutes it will have forgotten its original shape and be fairly obliging as you roll it out. You can force the dough to a given shape but it will probably tear and the surface of the bread will be rough and patchy.

Moulding bread dough can be undertaken in several different ways. The choice of method will depend on the size of the dough piece and the size of your hands. Moulding is normally done with both hands, this saves time and your right hand will follow your left in the moulding motion, or vice versa.

Moulding is best done on a wooden surface, or a kitchen work surface. Granite or marble are not recommended as they are cold and afford little grip for the dough. These surfaces if you have them are ideal for pastry work, but it is best to work on a wooden board.

The dough to be moulded should be covered with a damp cloth to avoid the surface skinning (drying out). If you find the dough has skinned apply a mist of water from your water spray, wait a moment and start moulding. Avoid too much flour on the surface or the dough as this will cause the dough to slide around and not grip the work surface.

To mould small items like rolls (petit pains), firstly imitate the claw and ball shape found on old furniture. Then, pressing gently on the dough with your hand, rotate the dough clockwise. The dough should be gently coiling up inside like an old clockwork spring. If you are moulding successfully the dough will be noticeably rounder, smoother and firmer. Moulding is like riding a push bike, it takes a little time and practice to perfect.

Larger bread units are moulded round by the use of the side of the hand curved into a crescent shape. Your hand pushes gently onto the sides of the dough piece and moves the dough forward as it rubs on the work surface. This is repeated until the dough is smooth and round.

3 strands for the plait

Start of a plait

Nearly finished plait

Dough can be flattened first and the ends folded in to form a rectangle. Having formed a rectangle of the desired length, the dough can be rolled up tightly. This is then rolled out to form a baguette or one strand of a plait.

I have seen dough shaped into a ball by taking a small amount of the outer edge of the dough to the centre. This is repeated several times until the ball is formed. The term "boulanger" is used for making balls of dough, a shape used long before the baguette. When the baguette is shaped as a long sausage you can if you wish angle your hands at 45° and roll them backwards and forwards on the ends to form a tapered end. This is also how you change a small ball of dough into the pointed ended petit pain. Your first attempts will not be to a professional standard, you can call it rustic if anyone asks! But never mind the shape, just enjoy the flavour.

You will find viewing the DVD useful as the moving demonstrations will, I trust, aid you to achieve perfection.

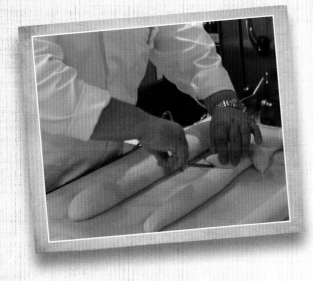

Le pain tresse

La couronne Bordelaise

Kid's Stuff

When in France I often stop to look in the Boulanger's window at the bread display. At the weekend there will be lots of regional speciality breads and creatures baked from dough. I have chosen four that you can make with children. They like to have them come in family groups; hedgehogs (*herisson*) come in large, medium and small. Snake (*serpent*), turtle, (*tortue marine*) and duck (*canard*) are all favourites with children.

First make up the dough and ferment it. 1kg of flour sized recipe will give you plenty of dough to make three hedgehogs and two other creatures. When the dough is fermented place it in the fridge to cool it down, an over active dough is difficult to handle. Take out enough dough to make your creature, keeping the dough covered with a damp tea cloth to prevent a skin forming.

Hedgehogs - weigh your family groups at 150g, 250g, and 350g of dough. Mould into balls, rest and roll one side of the ball forming it into a pear shape. Put some poppy seeds/linseeds onto a small plate. Masque the hedgehog's face with your hand and dampen the body with a spray or damp cloth. Roll the moist area (the body) into the poppy seeds or brown linseed and fully cover the body but not the face. Two ears may be snipped with scissors at the head and smaller snips all over the body to give the illusion of spines. Small feet can be applied if required, just roll out a piece of dough to the dimensions of a pencil. Cut into four, flatten both ends a little and tuck them under the body. The outer part of the foot can be cut to resemble toes.

A nose can be created by just touching the tip with water and dipping it into some poppy seed. Eyes are best applied after baking as currants tend to pop out in the oven. When the hedgehog is baked and still warm, make a little hole in the place for the eye and push a currant into each side of the head.

Aarix with Monsieur Herisson

Rosie with Madame Herisson

Neola with coiled snake

The Herisson Family

Snakes (scale at 350g) are long coiled up baguette shapes. A tapered tail end and a more rounded head should be created. A cut for the mouth and a forked tongue can be applied. Eyes are the same as for the hedgehog, with the snake's scales being snips with the scissors but cut then at an angle and laid flat by brushing them down with a finger.

Turtle (scale at 350g) is assembled very much like the hedgehog. Make a ball of dough and rest it. Then flatten the dough into a domed shape, apply four legs/feet and a snake head with no tongue. Again eyes are best applied after baking. Snakes and turtles can be coloured, use brown, yellow and green food colouring.

Place the creature in the oven for about 10 minutes and apply the colours to the snake and turtle in small rings, or diamonds. Small pots for the colours and a few water colour brushes need to be handy with a cup of water to wash your brushes in. Don't mix your colours or go from one colour to another. Return your creatures to the oven and fully bake them. *NB:* do not apply egg wash to any creature that is to be coloured as the food colour will not sink into any egg glazed surface.

Duck (scale at 350g) is an oval with a long neck (see diagram). The neck is first folded backwards over the body and then forwards again. The beak can be slightly flattened. A sharp knife can be used to create the wings, one shallow cut from behind the neck to the tail. Cuts can be made to define the wing feathers on the sides. This creature can be coloured or egg washed and baked. Eyes as with the other creatures applied after baking.

Finley and his turtle

If you use these basic techniques you can create more fun projects.

No animals have been harmed in the production of these creatures!

How to make the animals

Hedgehog

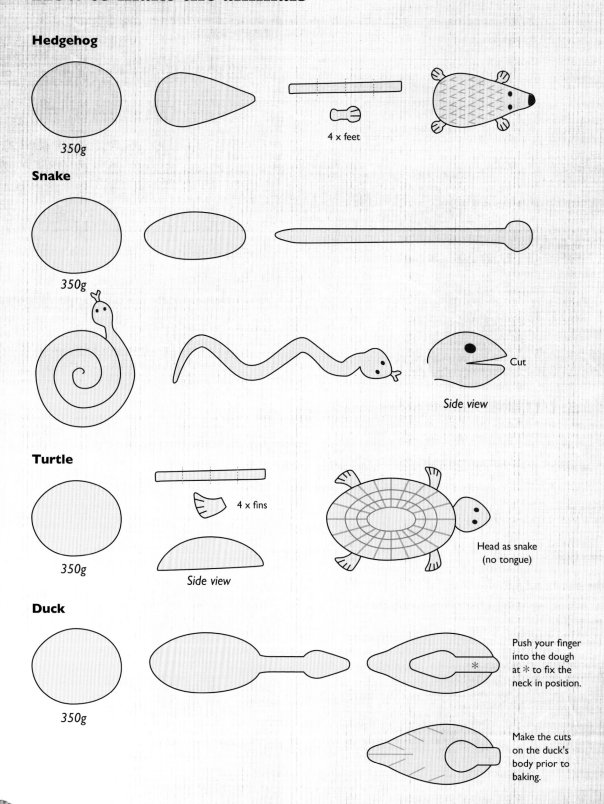

350g

4 x feet

Snake

350g

Cut

Side view

Turtle

4 x fins

Side view

350g

Head as snake
(no tongue)

Duck

350g

Push your finger
into the dough
at * to fix the
neck in position.

Make the cuts
on the duck's
body prior to
baking.

Bread Shapes

The term *Boulanger* was given to the bakers who made their loaves into round shapes (*boules*). This was the most popular shape up to the introduction of the *baguette*. This type of bread was linked to Vienna baking (with steam). Baking with steam gave a thinner crisp crust than that of the traditional dry baked boule. Long, cut breads like the *baguette* (drum stick) also have a bigger version, the *pain Parisienne* and a thinner one, the *ficelle* (boot lace). Shorter more compact breads are the long *bâtard*, short *bâtard* and *boulot*, all being baked with steam.

There are many different shapes and sizes of French breads available; the baguette is universal, other breads are regional and produced by the Artisan baker at "*Le Weekend*" or for festivals and holidays.

Some of the shapes found are linked to France's rustic past like the *tricorne* (a three sided hat) or the *tabatière* (a tobacco pouch). *Pain de Drôme* is inspired by the mountains, with *pain coupe epi retourné* being like waves. *Pain L'Auvergnat* is similar to our cottage loaf with a less generous top section.

Other shapes are achieved by plaiting and twisting the dough. The French baker shaped his dough first and placed it into a linen lined basket. This helped to keep the shape as it fermented and expanded. The proved dough was carefully tipped out onto the oven sole to bake.

In England, by the 1900s, bakers had abandoned many of the oven bottom breads as they were known. They adopted the bread tin which came in various shapes and sizes. The dough was placed into a prepared tin and proved, thus reducing handling and aiding mechanisation. British and French bakers chose different routes and there is little indication of a change of direction on either side of the Channel.

Four leaf clover

Shaping French Breads (Façonnage)

Baguette Shapes

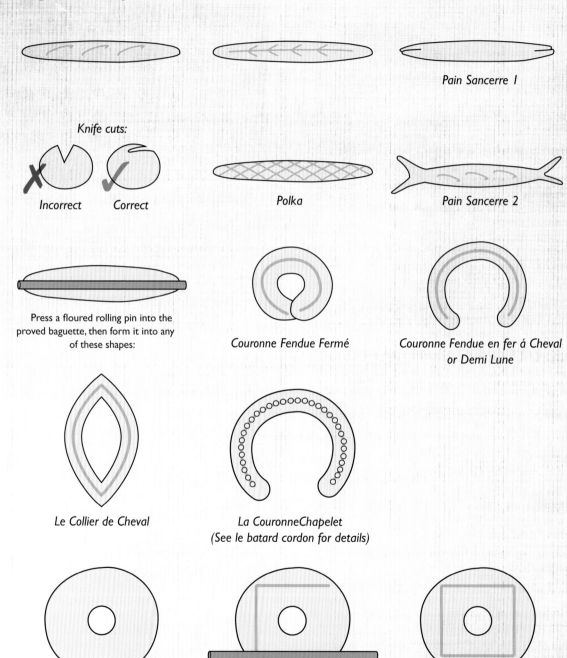

Pain Sancerre 1

Knife cuts:

Incorrect   Correct

Polka

Pain Sancerre 2

Press a floured rolling pin into the proved baguette, then form it into any of these shapes:

Couronne Fendue Fermé

Couronne Fendue en fer á Cheval or Demi Lune

Le Collier de Cheval

La CouronneChapelet
(See le batard cordon for details)

Roll out the dough flat, then make a hole in the centre with a cutter.

Prove on a flat tray or sheet (no edges if possible), then crease four times with a thin floured rolling pin.

La couronne fendue en quatre

Shaping French Breads (Façonnage)

Rugby Ball Shapes

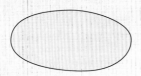

Pain au Maise 1

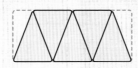

Leaves

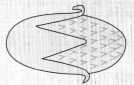

Pain au Maise 2

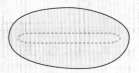

Form a crease, then moisten the top.

Roll out a thin spaghetti of dough.

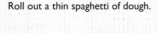

With a sawing action and the edge of your hand, form a line of pearls.

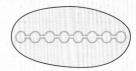

Le Bâtard Cordon

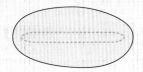

Form a crease, then moisten the top.

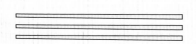

Form a 3 strand plait.
The strands should be $^1/_3$ longer than the loaf to allow for plaitting.

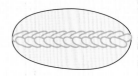

Pain avec Tresse
Similar to pain berch (2 strands)

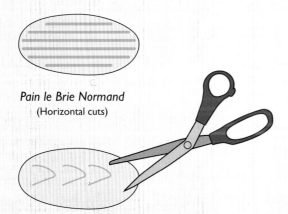

Pain le Brie Normand
(Horizontal cuts)

La Coupe épi Retournée
Cut deep ears of dough and then curl them over like waves.

Pain Serviette
(Vertical cuts)

Coupe épi Retourné side view

37

Shaping French Breads (Façonnage)

Rounds and Flat Oval Shapes

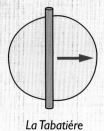

La Tabatiére

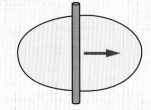

Flour and cut prior to baking.

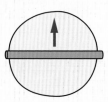

Keep centre raised.
Roll outwards to form a triangle.

Moisten surface and fold each point
into the centre.

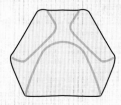

Le Tricorne

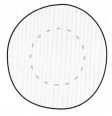

500g. Slightly flatten the ball top to allow
for expansion of the dough.

¹/10 (eg, 50g). Roll out to nearly
the size of the loaf.

Moisten and place the disc on top.
Push a finger down through the centre
of the dough to secure to the loaf.

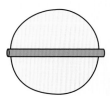

Flour and form crease. Prove upside
down and turn over for baking.

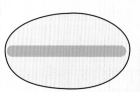

Le Pain Pistolet

Shaping French Breads (Façonnage)

Rounds

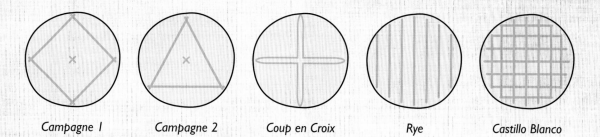

Campagne 1 Campagne 2 Coup en Croix Rye Castillo Blanco

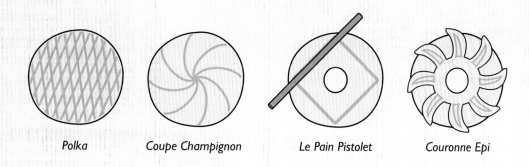

Polka Coupe Champignon Le Pain Pistolet Couronne Epi

Flat Ovals

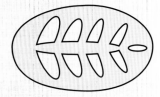

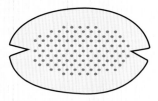

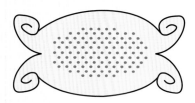

Fougasse
Can be made with an uncut base and
filled with ham and cheese.

Pimpean 1
Cut and pricked with a fork.

Pimpean 2
Cut, then ends teased out and rolled up
ready for leaves and cheese.

Bread Sizes and Weights Suitable for Home Baking

Because your domestic oven will have a tray size of approximately 38cm x 26cm you are restricted in what can be produced. It might be worth adding at this stage that most baking trays are four sided. Four sided trays tend to present problems when baking long breads like the bâtard and baguette. Getting the bâtard from the proving cloths and onto the tray is a nightmare, as the sides get in the way. The answer is to turn the tray over and use the base (no sides to get in the way). Care must be taken not to lose the dough off the tray as you transport it to the oven, ditto on removal from the oven. Baking on the underside of the tray also means if the bread has not baked fully on the base, you can slide the bread gently onto the oven shelf to finish off baking.

Baking on oven tiles

This gives you a base of heat on which to place the dough. It will be necessary to roll the bread onto a wooden slip. When on the slip cut and slide the dough onto the hot tile in the oven. Semolina on the slip will aid the movement of the dough from the slip to the tile. *NB:* This operation is dangerous as you could burn your hands if not very careful.

There should be no children or dogs around while you are working with the oven. Sleeves rolled down and use separate oven mitts. Because the tile holds lots of latent heat the bread dough will heat up, rapidly expanding along the cuts to give you that professional baked look. This achieves the best results but is not for the novice baker or children. You can bake up to 1.5kg of dough in an oval shape to maximise the oven/tray space, a sort of grande pain. I would suggest a diamond lattice cut (see "Pain Polka"). Most bread would be weighed at 500g - 600g.

General rules on bread baking

- Bake small breads at higher temperatures than large ones.

- Bread with sugar e.g. sucrose, lactose and honey need lower temperatures.

- Fruit breads need to be protected and baked at lower temperatures and for a longer time. Avoid 600g size fruit breads to start with.

- Croissants and products like brioche Litzellmann need a high initial oven temperature which gets the lift from the laminated layers, then the oven is turned down to avoid burning. This is also used for puff pastry.

Tray size: 38cm x 26 cm	Unbaked	Baked	Cuts	Length
1 Demi baguette	175g	125g	3/4	35cm
2 Ficelle	100g	80g	4	38cm
3 Long bâtard	350g	250g	4	38cm
4 Short bâtard	350g	250g	3	30cm
5 Petit pain	75g	50g	1	9cm
6 Boulot	350g	250g	2	25cm
7 Épi	180g	130g	4	36cm

Final Proof (or "Last Rising")

When the dough has been produced to the right consistency - weighed into units, shaped, rested and given a final shape, then and only then is the yeast given time to fully expand the envelope (bread dough). Un-leaven breads have little or no CO_2 gas inside to raise them. It is the trapped water that turns to steam expanding the un-leaven bread, pitta bread being a good example. Leaven bread is different; a matrix of tiny holes will have been created in mixing and through fermentation. It is these holes that will expand with gas produced by fermentation, thus lifting and expanding the dough.

Fermentation speeds are governed by available natural sugars occurring in the flour, the ambient temperature and, most importantly, the amount of time allocated for fermentation. Slow proving gives you plenty of time to react and less likelihood of over proving. Commercial provers in the UK are like a sauna, very warm and humid, proof times being 30 – 40 minutes. In France, bread will be put into a cool room, 5°C, overnight, where the dough will rise very slowly. Then, as and when required, the partially proved breads are brought out and brought up to the ambient temperature of the bakery. When fermentation speeds up from very slow to slow you will get a quality finished product. Baking takes place when the loaf is fully proved; taking the dough too early will result in poor shape and volume and a tendency for the loaf to split badly as it bakes.

Baguettes are best proved on your work surface in corrugations created in a tea cloth dusted with semolina. Round loaves are proved in baskets (*bannettes*) or plastic bowls with a tea cloth draped inside and again dusted with semolina flour. You can buy bannettes in France, though they can be expensive and you could improvise and adapt baskets produced for other purposes. With this method of proof the dough piece is placed in the basket or corrugation upside down, i.e. the top part of the moulded dough top side down. When tipped or roll gently out they are the right side up. The bannette is used to support the proving dough piece; if not, the soft dough would flow out and no longer be a ball, but rather a flat disc! The fully proved dough must be cut immediately with a razor sharp blade and placed in a preheated oven along with a bowl or tray of boiling water in the bottom. If the ambient temperature in your kitchen should decrease, proof time will increase. Do not worry if the dough takes longer; unless you have a dead line it's not a problem. If you need to speed up the process, try the cupboard with the heating boiler or some other warm place.

Dough is considered to be proved when it is about double its original volume. If you lightly touch the newly moulded dough with your finger tip it will resist, the part you have touched will spring back. When the dough is ripe and ready to bake, the dough does not spring back when touched with your finger.

Unless you have a constant temperature in your kitchen there will be variations in proof times, longer in winter and perhaps a little shorter in summer. Time and experience will tell you when the dough is just right for baking. If you have space for a small extra fridge in your kitchen, it could be used to hold retarded dough. Set the refrigerator at the warmest setting about 4-5°C. You can hold your unproved bread doughs over night. The dough may need to be covered with polythene or sprayed with a mist of water to avoid the surface drying out. Then they can be removed and allowed to prove at ambient kitchen temperatures.

The fully fermented dough must be processed carefully. As soon as you roll out your baguette gently place it on to the tray or tile, it must be decorated with seeds and cut and placed in the oven all in one seamless operation. Make sure you have all the required equipment and ingredients to hand, as delay after cutting will cause the dough to collapse. So spray, decorate with seeds, cut, open the pre-heated oven (step back to avoid the steam) and carefully place your trays in the oven. There should be some extra expansion in the oven about 10%, called oven spring. This expansion can be seen in the cuts on a baguette, they will open up and without these cuts the loaf would split down its length. Final proof is also called last rising or second fermentation, *l'appret.*

Decorative Cutting

Cutting bread is important, as the cut guarantees expansion along and through the cut. A baguette without its cuts would split and tear along one of the long sides of the loaf, most often making it unsightly.

Cutting bread in a particular style will identify its type, region and, in the past, even a specific baker. Bread dough is generally cut at an angle of 30° which creates a flap. This cut will give the recognisable shape of the classic baguette Française. Cutting can be done with a razor, craft knife or, for some styles like pain épi, scissors are used.

Fougasse (oven bread) is flat bread that is further cut to aid even baking. The final iconic shape is achieved by rolling, shaping and cutting.

The supermarket has removed many of the small village bakers from bread manufacturing. This in turn has reduced the range of artisan breads available but the French bakers are fighting back and still maintain a market share through open air markets and their shops.

Finally, the contrast between the baked dough and the cut surface can be further enhanced by the use of flour and seed dressings.

In order to keep seeds adhered to the dough surface you can:

- Shape and then roll the dough in seeds. If the surface of the dough has dried then spray a mist of water on the dough first. This gives a coating of seeds.

- Prove the dough, spray with water and sprinkle with seeds, this gives a light coating of seeds. Then wait a few minutes to allow the surface of the dough to skin a little and cut with a sharp wet knife or razor.

- Flour can be used to decorate the top of bread and rye is best as it will not brown as quickly as wheat flour. The use of rye and semolina maintain the contrast between the dressing and the baked dough. Semolina can also be used in this way. Bread is then cut prior to baking.

- Seeds and nuts going on top of unbaked bread should not be toasted prior to use. This is done for seeds going inside the dough to enhance their flavour.

Me at the Paris Bakery School

Baking the Perfect Crusty Loaf

Crisp, crusty bread is what we have learned to expect from the French bread bakeries. Some items like brioche and viennoiseries are not considered to be bread, and are not crusty by design. Also there are soft breads like Pain au Lait available. It's not everyone's idea of fun to have one's palette scratched raw by crusty bread and rolls. Crust characteristics are varied by the use of steam/water vapour in the oven. Baking a boule or pavé without steam will result in a thick crust being formed.

Many of the traditional country breads are still baked on the oven sole, with a little humidity present. This then was the old traditional baking method used throughout France. Then along came a new method of baking from Vienna. This involved injecting water or casting water on the oven sole to produce steam, **not to be used in modern ovens!**

The reason for creating steam in the oven was so that the super heated vapour would condense on the surface of the dough. For this to work the steam needs a cold surface, like steamy windows in winter. Heat is then exchanged with the dough. The surface dough gelatinises and gives the bread its thin crust. This was a great success for the bakers, as their customers loved this type of bread. It was a welcome change from the fairly tough thick crust on the old traditional breads.

Special ovens were built with sloping oven soles. These were built with soles at an angle of about 30° in order that the steam would not rush back out of the oven door. The steam stayed in the oven, creating the much sought after thin crisp crust. Towards the end of the baking period, a small trap door (damper) in the side of the oven was opened. By expelling the steam the bread crust dried and became crisp. Failure to remove the steam would result in a loaf or baguette looking fine on removal from the oven but on cooling it would become soft, tough and rubbery, having lost all of its desirable characteristics. Placing warm baguettes in a polythene bag will cause the same thing to happen. This is why in France bread is transported warm by hand or in a cotton sack made for this purpose.

Commercial ovens are constructed with steam injection or water to steam systems built in. At home you can make some steam by placing a small baking tin with boiling water in it at the bottom of the oven.

Bread dough can also be sprayed with water on entry to the oven. Bake for approximately 2/3 of the baking cycle time with steam, then open the oven door (step back) and let the steam and hot gasses out (make sure the kitchen is fully ventilated). Remove the water container with care and bake for the last 1/3 to fully bake the bread. Remove from the oven, place on a wire tray to cool and within thirty seconds of removal from the oven, mist spray the bread with a little water.

A well baked loaf should develop tiny eggshell like cracks on the surface of the bread. Often you can hear the sound of bread crackling as it cools. Bread should be fully cooled before it is stored. Steam baked crust must be allowed to breathe.

Storage of this type of bread should be in permeable or perforated bags. To freshen up this type of bread, run the uncut bread under the tap, and then place it in a preheated hot oven or grill. Consume immediately, as like toast it will not be good cold.

Ovens

Types: Gas, Electric, Solid Fuel and Microwaves

Baking is a form of cooking, heat circulates around the cabinet (a box) and makes the bread edible by the application of heat. Heat is conducted through the tray into the base of the bread, this is why oven tiles are wonderful to bake on. Heat is also radiated from the top of the oven, down onto the bread below. Between the conducted and radiated heat the loaf is baked. Some humidity in the oven will help the dough expand in the early stage of baking. Domestic ovens don't have steam facilities as standard so you must place a water bath inside your oven at the bottom.

Commercial ovens have heat controls on both the top and the bottom, so it is possible to have a low top heat setting eg 180°C and 220°C on the bottom. Domestic ovens can give you the option of having the top heat off and the bottom one on. It is possible to shut the top heat off part way through the bake or perhaps place some form of mask over the bread to protect it from the top heat e.g. with fruit breads or some types of brioche.

Many ovens are installed in combinations of main oven, oven/grill and a microwave oven above, these are in housing units. Don't let anyone have your kitchen designed with the oven next to the freezer, they look good on paper. Freezers and oven compete for heat and cold, the ovens heat exhaust will disrupt the freezer/fridges ability to cool itself down.

There is not much difference between gas and electric for baking. Gas is perhaps a little moister inside the oven, as water is given off as part of the burning of gas. You will still need a water bath in the base of your oven.

Fan assisted ovens are worth thinking about if you plan to buy a new oven. The fan pushes the hot air around the oven giving all baked goods a shorter baking time at a lower temperature. I think this could be energy saving. Non fan assisted ovens tend to have layers of heat, with hot at the top and the temperature becomes lower on the middle and bottom shelves. So you may be guessing the temperature you have in your oven, not a good start. Get an oven thermometer - you will hear this from me again. Put the thermometer in the oven, set the oven at 200°C and see what the thermometer reads inside the oven. They can be 30°C over or under and this will ruin all your attempts to produce a good loaf.

Oven quality - if you are fortunate enough to be able to buy yourself a new oven, make sure you get a good one. You can tell if it is well made by looking at the door. If the door is heavy and fairly thick in width and feels firm and well engineered, then the oven will be of a similar quality. It is worth having a look at my DVD for further tips.

Microwave ovens don't bake bread unless they are combination types. This is because the microwave system cooks from the inside of the loaf and would not give you the caramelised outer crust and very little of the anticipated bread taste and characteristics we enjoy. Microwaves are useful for melting and heating fondants, glazes, and syrups, but then that's just my opinion.

Hot plates and griddles are the great grandparents of ovens, and in some cases will do a better job of baking ethnic flat breads. This is a high temperature short time process, so galettes and crêpes can be produced without an oven.

Oven tiles at home

Cooling Bread

It is important that all beads are fermented products
are removed from trays and baking tins immediately
on removal from the oven. Bread should be cooled on
a wire tray, with ample air circulation and stored when
cold. If French bread is allowed to sweat it will lose its
characteristic crustiness.

Traditional French bread is stored in baskets and
transported in a cloth sack.

Section Two

Baie de Somme · Abbeville
Amiens
Rouen · Beauvais
Bayeux
Paris · Versailles
Le Mont Saint-Michel · Argentan · Chartres
Orléans
Chatillon sur Loire
Angers · Sancerre
Brissac-Quincé, · Saumur
Château Pimpean
Poitiers · Moulins
Saint Étienne
Nevers sur Loire
Limoges
Valence
Argentat · Crest · Die
Villefranche · Vercheny
Cahors · Flaviac
Lanuéjouls
Avignon · Trigance
Nîmes · Arles
Toulouse
Pau
Carcassonne · Narbonne

Recipes and Places:

Forty recipes from along the Pilgrim's routes through France

Amiens

St Honoré the Pilgrims route

Amiens is a northern French city with whom Honoré had strong links. That in mind, I went to visit the museum library for more information on the Patron Saint of Bakers and Pastry Chefs. The city was partially destroyed in the Grande Guerre and like so many, it has its share of modern functional buildings that could easily be seen in a city like Sheffield. We drove around looking for somewhere to park our car; I spotted a leafy square off the main auto-route and turned into it. Fate must have had its hand on the tiller that day because it was the rue St Honoré and there was a parking place for us! After a drink at a local café we set off to find out about Honoré the man. Walking towards the city centre we passed the front of a biscuit factory, long since closed. The front entrance to the building is decorated with ceramic tiles depicting childhood scenes in the Art Nouvelle style. The entrance is a work of art and should you find yourself in the area, do go and see it - it is a hidden gem.

We headed in to the city and it was clear from the damage to many of the principal buildings that a war had been fought here. The few older buildings that had the good fortune to remain showed that this city had not been spared the horrors of war. The library had taken several hits, deep holes caused by artillery shells marked the walls, and luckily, this had been saved and later restored for the future. Here the librarian was most helpful and supplied books and articles. These would help us in our quest to find more about Bishop Honoré the man.

Honoré came from a wealthy family with servants and it is due to one of the servants that the link between Honoré and the bakers was forged. The story goes that young Honoré who was by all accounts a bit of a lad, was promised to the church. The servant who overheard his mother's joyous remarks, said, as she removed the fresh baked bread from the oven, " If young Honoré makes good in the church, this peel will take root and bring forth fruit". The servant took the peel and sank it into the ground. The peel took root flowering annually and there were regular visits from believers to his home. There are many and varied accounts of his life, including fasting and recovering holy relics, to name but a few. I chose the one about the peel, because I can believe most of it.

Honoré was made Bishop of Amiens and later, because of his evangelising work, became a saint. I have not found any record of his travels and so the journeys are not historical facts, they are folklore and contain a generous portion of poetic licence. There are recorded pilgrim routes, so I have taken these and combined them with a visit to the Pope. I know of his need to meet the people, so I think he might have chosen to travel and preach. It was on this basis that I made my

choice of his route. There are one or two deviations and some opportunities for debating historical accuracy.

The bakers in Paris took Honoré as their Patron Saint and one of the gates into Paris was given his name. It was at this gate that Joan the Maid of Orléans met her fate, wounded, she was captured and handed over to the English and the rest is history.

I first came across St. Honoré at the Paris Bakery School in Bercy. His carved wooden image has him standing with a Crosier and Peel together in his hand. There are carvings and stained glass windows bearing his image in France. He is also remembered at the Cathedral in Amiens. His head along with other hundreds of saints and bishops can be found in cathedral entrances.

To be a pilgrim was most important to every Christian in medieval Europe, to visit holy sites with relics was a life's aim. Honoré travelled and evangelised at the same time and he visited many locations as he preached to the masses. France was then a number of Duchies often at war with each other, or the English or perhaps both. Travel by the Peage or Route National was out of the question, as cart tracks would be all there was. The super highway was the river and resting places would be walled towns or fortifications. As pilgrimages became more popular, more Monasteries and Chantrys sprang up along the way, villages upgraded to towns and being on the pilgrim's route or having a Saints relic would bring wealth and status to a town.

Santiago de Compostela in Spain was the ultimate place for the medieval pilgrim to visit. It was a long distance to travel. St Honoré might have taken the overland route from Amiens to Orléans via Beavais and Paris, (not the capital then) to the river Loire for some of the journey.

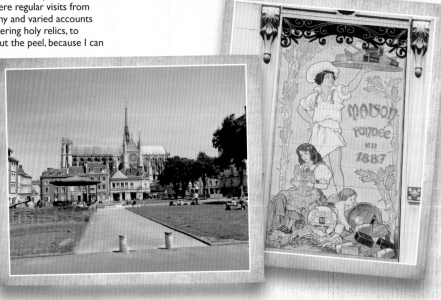

La Boule Fendue en Croix

Ingredients

400g	White bread flour
100g	Sieved malted flour*
175g	Levain
5g	Yeast fresh
8g	Salt
10g	Butter (optional)
310g	Water

Total weight: 1.08kg

Sieve out any malted grains from a malted wheat bread flour

Dough temp:	21°C
Mixing water temp:	_____°C
1st speed mix time:	6 mins
2nd speed mix time:	6 + 4 (or 16/18 mins by hand)
1st fermentation time:	3 hours
Conditions:	Cool and covered
De-gas/knock back:	90 mins
Scale at:	500g
Yield:	2
Resting period:	10 mins
Tray tin type and size:	2 sheet trays
Warm/prepare:	Lightly oiled
Shape and form dough:	2 boules
Prove at:	25°C for 60 mins +
Pre-baking finish:	Dust with a little flour, flatten, make a cross
Oven temperature:	220°C (fan 210°C)
Baking time:	40/50 mins
Conditions:	With humidity
Post baking finish:	None

Approximate production time: 4 hours
Product life: 2 days

Mixing Method (levain-levure)

- Place the dry ingredients in a bowl, (reserve the salt with 15g of water for the second stage).
- Put yeast, water and levain in a mixing bowl, mix for 6 minutes on 1st speed, then mix for a further 6 minutes on 2nd speed.
- Stop and add the salt and water to the dough mix for 4 minutes.
  N.B. if mixing by hand add the salt with the flour.
- Mix for 16-18 minutes.
- Cover and ferment for 3 hours.
- De-gas after 90 minutes and cover.
- After 3 hours scale 2 units at 500g.
- Mould round and rest for 10 minutes.
- Re-mould and place on a baking sheet with adequate space for expansion.
- Prove for 1 hour.
- Place into the oven as soon as possible and bake.
- Flour and then press down hard on the dough with a thin rolling pin or a short section of a broom handle to make a cross.

Beauvais

This is a famous town with history going back to 1099. It was the origin of the people's revolt in 1357. In the 1600s the town was famed for its inventors and philosophers. The association with medieval builders is the part of this town's history that intrigues me. In the year 1225 the Bishop of Beauvais set out to build the biggest and tallest cathedral of its day.

The building work was completed in A.D. 1263. It had several setbacks in construction as the project had exceeded the builders' knowledge of load bearing foundations. The Cathedral developed stress fractures and collapsed in A.D. 1272. The expression "on your head be it" might have been uttered just before the collapse.

The vault was rebuilt but the weight distribution was not fully understood and it fell down again. More strength to the foundations of the buttresses was needed. The use of the flying buttresses was found to be the solution. Now the weight of the vast vaulted naves of the Norman Cathedrals could be supported. Check out the Cathedral of Notre Dame in Paris for some fine examples of flying buttresses.

This snatched view of history is fascinating enough to have had a novel written about it, and even a mini series for TV. The facts of this tale revolved around the Cathedral of Saint Pierre and its building. The foundations of this ecclesiastical building developed into an architectural proving ground for all French builders in the future.

Beauvais has plenty of artisan bakers and the regional breads are available on the bakers' stalls at the open air and covered markets.

Pastry Chefs have had their moments with construction and foundations. Wedding cakes for the Royals would often be up to seven tiers high. Weight distribution and height has resulted in the higher tiers tumbling at the most inopportune moments. The introduction of tiers on pillars required steel plates to be introduced into base cakes or the use of decorated boxes for the upper tiers to reduce the load.

One of the Cathredral's Gargoyles

Le Pain Régence

Ingredients

450g	White bread flour
50g	Rye flour
8g	Yeast fresh
8g	Salt
5g	Fat (optional)
305g	Water + tsp of treacle
180g	Pre-fermented dough (18 hours)

Total weight: 1.06kg

Mixing Method (directe)

- Place all the ingredients in the bowl except the salt and the pre-fermented dough.
- Mix slowly for 5 minutes
- Make a paste with the salt and 15g of hot water taken from the recipe.
- Add the pre-fermented dough and the salt paste to the bread dough.
  N.B. If mixing by hand add the salt with the flour.
- Mix for a further 10 minutes on 2nd speed.
- By hand mix for 20 minutes.
- When mixed cover the dough and set aside for 2 hours.
- De-gas after 1 hour, and cover.
- After 2 hours de-gas and scale into 5 x 50g pieces
- Rest and mould into balls
- Spray the dough with water and roll in sesame and poppy seeds forming an arc, with alternating seeds.
- Place on a prepared tray
- Cover and prove for 45 minutes then bake

Dough temp:	22°C
Mixing water temp:	_____°C
1st speed mix time:	5 mins
2nd speed mix time:	10 mins (or 20 mins by hand)
1st fermentation time:	2 hours
Conditions:	Ambient and covered
De-gas/knock back:	1 hour
Scale at:	250g
Yield:	5
Resting period:	10 mins
Tray tin type and size:	38cm x 26cm tray
Warm/prepare:	Lightly greased
Shape and form dough:	Divide into 5 balls
Prove at:	25°C for 45 mins
Pre-baking finish:	spray balls of dough with water, roll in alternate seeds,
Oven temperature:	230°C (fan 220°C)
Baking time:	20 mins
Conditions:	With humidity for 15 mins
Post baking finish:	Lightly spray with water

Approximate production time: 3 hours
Product life: 2 days

Paris

The area where Paris stands was first used by Gallic fishermen. They built a small settlement by the Seine, trading fish for anything they needed. The Romans followed and built on both banks and stayed to build a town. The remains of the Roman baths and the amphitheatre are still to be seen on the south bank of the river.

In the third century, Saint Denis, the first Bishop of Paris was killed by the Barbarian hordes; they also burned the town down, because that is what barbarians do. Along came Genevieve who helped the inhabitants to safety and saved them from the hordes, that's how she became a saint.

In 508 AD, Clovis, King of the Franks settled in Paris and founded an Abbey to St Genevieve. Some years later in 885 AD the Norsemen sailed up the Seine and laid siege to Paris, this upset the locals greatly. Eudes, son of Robert the Strong recruited an army of local folk and drove the Norsemen out. For this he was made King of France and Paris became a Royal seat. Unfortunately the Norsemen came back on several occasions, burning the original Abbey of Saint Germain and Abbey Church of Saint Denis.

Not to be deterred, Abbot Suger rebuilt the Abbey Church of Saint Denis and many more august buildings. I think this was an ecclesiastic two fingers sign to the Barbarians and the Norsemen. Perhaps he said "You're fired".

Bread is still a very important commodity to the Parisiennes, so there are plenty of Artisan bakers around.

Foodies buy Pain Biologic and the Algerians and Tunisians purchase their flat breads. The big baguette *pain Parisienne* is always available and eating it in the park as part of a picnic with my students was a memorable moment. If you take a walk down the streets you will find lots of interesting versions of classic breads, like cheese and ham filled and baked Fougasse.

My choice of bread for Paris is Pain de Paris, aimed at professional people who need flavour and roughage in their diet. This is special bread for a special city.

La Madeleine Paris

Parisian Patisserie

Cheese and Ham

Pain de Paris

Ingredients

275g	White bread flour
150g	Spelt flour
75g	Wheat bran
60g	Golden linseed
175g	Levain
10g	Sea salt
325g	Water
10g	Yeast fresh

Total weight: 1.8kg

Dough temp:	26°C
Mixing water temp:	_____°C
1st speed mix time:	10 mins
2nd speed mix time:	5 mins (or 20 mins by hand)
1st fermentation time:	2 hours
Conditions:	22°C covered
De-gas/knock back:	After 1 hour
Scale at:	500g
Yield:	2
Resting period:	10 mins
Tray tin type and size:	Long bread tin (warm/prepared)
Shape and form dough:	Into bâtards
Prove at:	25°C
Pre-baking finish:	Multi-grain dressing
Oven temperature:	230°C (fan 220°C)
Baking time:	35 mins
Conditions:	Humidity throughout the bake
Post baking finish:	Mist spray with water exiting the oven

Approximate production time: 3 hours
Product life: 2 days

Mixing Method (levain-levure)

Stage 1
- Pre-soak the bran and linseed for 30 minutes with 100g of tepid water from the recipe.

Stage 2
- Place the dry ingredients including the sea salt in the mixing bowl along with the levain, yeast and water.
- Mix for 30 seconds then add the pre-soaked bran and linseed.
- Mix for 10 minutes 1st speed, then 5 minutes 2nd speed.
- By hand 20 minutes.
- Cover and set aside for 2 hours.
- After 1 hour de-gas and cover.
- After 2 hours scale into 2 x 500g units and mould round.
- Rest for 10 minutes
- Mould into bâtards, the same length as your loaf tin.
- Place the bâtard into a prepared loaf tin, lightly spray with water.
- Sprinkle with a mixed seed dressing
- Prove for 40-50 minutes or double the original size.
- Bake for 35 minutes with humidity.

53

Versailles

The events that led to the French Revolution crystallised at the gates of the Palace of Versailles. Starvation stalked the streets, hundreds died each week, and the people of Paris ate rats and dogs in order to stay alive.

Bakers in their desperation to find material for bread used peas, beans and seeds mixed with the little flour there was. Ground animal bones and sweepings from the mill all found their way into the bread, which was as dreadful as the lives of the poor Parisians.

Whether Queen Marie Antoinette d' Autriche even uttered the infamous words, *"Qu'ils mangent de la brioche"* ("Let them eat cake" in English), perhaps the use of them by the revolutionaries was politically inspired mischief designed to tarnish the Queen's already fading popularity. Despite the fact that she probably never even said those unfortunate words, they appeared to illustrate just how little she knew or cared about her starving people's plight.

The French people took their Queen's indiscretion to heart: she was, after all, just an Austrian upstart and she became the focus of their hatred. The suggestion that, if they did not have bread, they should make do with brioche, a confection of eggs, butter and flour beyond the wildest dreams of most of the people, was politically disastrous. The bread for Versailles therefore has to be brioche.

Entrance to Versailles

Petit Trianon

Distant View of Petit Trianon

Pain Brioche (Savoury Brioche)

Ingredients

500g	Strong white flour
240g	Water
18g	Yeast fresh
7g	Salt
8g	Sugar
10g	Milk powder
3g	Malt extract or treacle
40g	Butter
50g	Large egg (one)
10g	Lemon juice
160g	Pre-fermented dough

Total weight: 1.46kg

Dough temp:	26°C
Mixing water temp:	_____°C
1st speed mix time:	3 mins
2nd speed mix time:	10mins (or 20 mins by hand)
1st fermentation time:	45 mins
Conditions:	Warm and covered
De-gas/knock back:	30 mins
Scale at:	500g
Yield:	2
Resting period:	20 mins
Tray tin type and size:	Large loaf tins 22cm x 11cm
Warm/prepare:	Lightly greased
Shape and form dough:	Into long rolls to fit tins
Prove at:	25°C for 60 mins
Pre-baking finish:	Egg/milk wash, sprinkle with sesame or poppy seeds
Oven temperature:	200°C (fan 190°C)
Baking time:	40 mins
Conditions:	Small amount of steam for the whole of the bake
Post baking finish:	None

Approximate production time: 3 hours
Product life: 5 days

Mixing Method (directe)

- Place the flour, salt, milk powder and butter into a mixing bowl.
- Put tepid water, treacle, sugar, yeast, lemon juice and egg in a jug. Stir for 2 minutes
- Pour the liquid into the bowl with the dry ingredients.
- Mix for 5 minutes slow speed or by hand forming dough.
- Rest for 5 minutes.
- Add the pre-fermented dough.
- Mix for 10 minutes on medium speed (by hand 20 minutes.)
- Cover and ferment for 45 minutes
- De-gas after 30 minutes.
- After 45 minutes scale at 500g x 2 and mould
- Rest for 20 minutes.
- Mould the dough into a bâtard to fit the loaf tins. Alternatively, use a brioche tin, or form a plait.
- Cover and prove for 1 hour in a warm room.
- Pre-bake finish.
- Bake with humidity for 40 minutes.

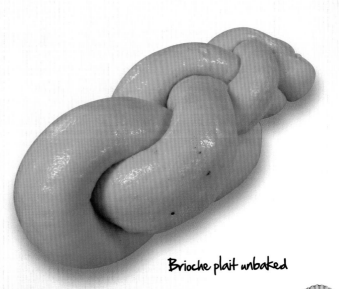

Brioche plait unbaked

Chartres

Chartres has been a place of worship since the dawn of time. Druids, Romans and Pagans all chose this area as it was thought the natural springs were holy. The Romans settled here and called the town Autricium taking the name from the river Autura, now known as the Eure. The springs once honoured by followers of the Goddess Sulis Minerva were rededicated to the Virgin Mary when Christianity arrived.

The first cathedral on this site was burned by the Norsemen in 858, and then they returned again to besiege the city in 911, without success. The construction of the new cathedral started in 1205 and finished in 1271. It is a most magnificent building. Because of its location the building could be seen by travellers from miles around and would be used to help them navigate around the country.

The English gained the city in battle in 1417 and lost it again in 1432, the occupants of Chartres being glad to see them go. French Protestants attacked the city in 1568 but the Catholic garrison held firm and the Protestant attempt at taking the city failed. In the Franco-Prussian war Chartres was occupied by the Germans, who liked it so much they returned again in 1940.

In 1944, Chartres was bombed by the United States Air Force, who fortunately missed the Cathedral. It was suggested by U.S. army intelligence (a contradiction in terms) that the Germans were using Chartres Cathedral as an observation post, so the Americans were planning to bomb it just in case. US Colonel Welborn Barton Griffith, Jr. stuck his neck out and said "Hold on, don't bomb it just yet." He and another soldier visited the Cathedral and found that the Germans had not used the place for any military purpose, so it was spared. Sadly Colonel Griffith was killed about a month later. The Chartres area is famous for growing wheat, flour milling, artisan breads and game pies.

The knave

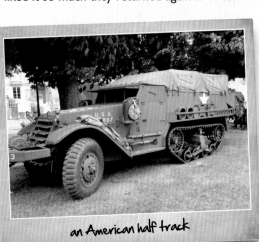

an American half track

Baguette ready for the shop

La Baguette Française

Ingredients

Poolish

125g	White bread flour
125g	Water (38°C)
2g	Yeast fresh

Total 252g

Dough

438g	White bread flour
250g	Water
5g	Yeast fresh
8g	Salt

Total weight: 953g

Poolish temp:	38°C
Dough temp:	23°C
Mixing water temp:	_____ °C
1st speed mix time:	5 mins
2nd speed mix time:	12 mins (or 20 mins by hand)
1st fermentation time:	90 mins
Conditions:	Ambient and covered
De-gas/knock back:	45 mins
Scale at:	175g
Yield:	5
Resting period:	10 mins
Tray tin type and size:	Baking tile or trays
Shape and form dough:	Demi baguettes
Prove at:	20°C for 75 mins
Pre-baking finish:	3-4 cuts on the top surface at an angle then place immediately in the oven
Oven temperature:	240°C (fan 230°C)
Baking time:	15 mins
Conditions:	Tray with a little boiling water in the bottom of the oven for 12 mins of baking period. Then the oven needs venting to remove the steam.

Approximate production time: 5 hours 30 mins
Product life: 1 day

Mixing Method (fabrication sur poolish)

- Mix the flour, water and yeast and place in a container with plenty of room for expansion.

- Cover and set aside in a warm place for 3 hours.

- Mix all the ingredients except the salt with the poolish for 5 minutes.

- Pause for 5 minutes .

- Then add the salt softened with 10g of hot water from the recipe and mix for 12 minutes.

- Cover and ferment for 90 minutes.

- De-gas after 45 minutes.

- Scale at 175g and shape round.

- Rest for 10 minutes and shape into demi baguettes.

- Place on a floured linen tea towel formed into corrugations to hold the baguettes.

- Cover and prove for 75 minutes.

- Roll onto a wooden slip, cut and transfer to the oven tile immediately.

Orléans

Orléans was once the capital of France. It is situated on a bend in the river Loire and this, with its proximity to the fertile plains around Beauce to the north, made it important. The years 1428 to 1429 found the city under siege by the English. The Earl of Salisbury needed to take the bridge in order to join forces with other English armies located to the north and south of the city. Enter Joan of Arc, the darling of the French forces, who arrived ahead of her main battle group and put the fear of God into the besieging forces. On the 8th of May 1429 Salisbury's forces capitulated and a legend was born. *Le Pain de Campagne* is a fitting bread for Joan of Arc, who was a woman from a rural background.

Bishop Honoré would have passed through the port of Orléans on his way south. Modern day Orléans still has a feeling of importance, boasting lots of important and impressive buildings which line leafy squares and parks. Keen to avoid the city traffic, we ventured into the city on a Sunday morning in June.

Central Orléans has a large flea market, with ample parking available, thankfully. We stopped and toured the market. Everything was there, from Persian rugs to antique bread baskets, called bannette. I returned with souvenirs from the Great War, having nearly purchased a set of antique bread shop scales, but resisted the temptation as I have a kitchen already full of bread-related memorabilia. Orléans is still home to plenty of artisan bakers but sadly, as with many large town and cities, supermarkets are squeezing them out.

The Loire

Wild flowers

Pain de Campagne sur Levain (Country Bread)

Ingredients

350g	Levain
450g	Bread flour
50g	Rye flour
315g	Water
2g	Yeast fresh
10g	Salt*
8g	Butter

Total 1.185kg

Mixing Method

- Place flours, water, yeast, butter, and levain in a bowl, do not add salt yet.
  (If mixing by hand, add the salt)

- Mix slowly for 8 minutes now add salt (*which has been softened in 10g of hot water).

- Mix for another 8 minutes slowly.
  (If mixing by hand, 20 minutes)

- Place the dough in a suitable sized bowl to allow for expansion, cover the dough.

- Ferment for 2 hours

- After 1 hour de-gas, cover.

- After a further hour remove and scale at 390g. Mould round.

- Rest for 10 minutes and then form into boules.

- Place onto a warmed, lightly greased tray.

- Prove for 90 minutes.

- Pre-baking finish lightly floured and shallow cut, and then place immediately into a pre-heated oven with humidity.

Levain temp:	21°C
Dough temp:	°C
1st speed mix time:	8 mins
2nd speed mix time:	8 mins (or 20 mins by hand)
1st fermentation time:	2 hours
Conditions:	Warm and covered
De-gas/knock back:	1 hour
Scale at:	390g
Yield:	3
Resting period:	10 mins
Tray tin type and size:	38cm x 26cm
Warm/prepare:	Lightly greased
Shape and form dough:	Into bâtards
Prove at:	25°C for 90 mins
Pre-baking finish:	Flour and cut 3 times diagonally (shallow cuts)
Oven temperature:	230°C (fan 210°C)
Baking time:	25 - 30 mins
Conditions:	With steam for 20 mins
Post baking finish:	None

Approximate production time: 3 hours
Product life: 2 days

Chatillon sur Loire

A small town on the pilgrims' route south, this was a natural fording place to cross the river. It is still a crossing point and serves the rural economy as a market town. The ancient part of the town is built on the hill side where a small amount of renovation is taking place. The town has an interesting museum with an exhibition of Neolithic and Gallo-Roman finds alongside articles of feminine apparel from the 1800s.

The tourist trade breathed new life into Chatillon with the introduction of a mini port. Here there are facilities for repairs and hiring barges. A park with picnic tables and an auberge are close to the berths and these provide a pleasant place to moor for the night. The marina supplies important services, water and electricity to the many barges that navigate the waterways.

this, it's park, purchase and go - no time to chat!

The Froments are traditional bakers producing regional breads and specialist gateaux and pastries for the town's folks and passing nautical tourists. Christophe employs two members of staff; his baker and a female apprentice patissiere.

His apprentice attends college and will soon finish her studies after taking her examinations. The shop is run by Sandrine and in between schooling, her son helps out too. The shop bell never stops ringing as people enter and exit the shop on Rue Martial Vuldet. Pain Christophe is of my creation by way of a thank you for the help and kindness I received.

Christophe, Sandrine and myself

There are four or five bakeries in Chatillon, some are only shop fronts supplied from a bakery unit out of town. Others still bake on the premises. One such is Boulangerie Le Pain de Vie, the home and work place of Sandrine and Christophe Froment and family. Christophe's bakery is located on the narrow approach leading to the canal bridge. Parking outside his shop is limited to 5 minutes only. As a result of

A view along the canal

Wall paintings

Pain Fournil de Christophe

Ingredients

150g	White bread flour
150g	Brown bread flour
200g	Rye flour
175g	Pre-ferment dough (18 hours)
15g	Butter
12g	Salt
10g	Yeast fresh
2g	Ground cumin
65g	Raisins
350g	Water & dark beer (50:50)
2g	Pumpkin seeds

Total 1.131kg

Dough temp:	25°C
Mixing water temp:	_____°C
1st speed mix time:	6 mins
2nd speed mix time:	14 mins
1st fermentation time:	2 hours
Conditions:	Warm, ambient and covered
De-gas/knock back:	1 hour
Scale at:	560g
Yield:	2
Resting period:	10 mins
Tray tin type and size:	38 x 26cm
Warm/prepare:	Lightly greased
Shape and form dough:	Boule or short bâtard
Prove at:	25°C for 90 mins
Pre-baking finish:	Spray with water and sprinkle with pumpkin seeds
Oven temperature:	210°C (fan 200°C)
Baking time:	40 mins
Conditions:	with humidity for 35mins
Post baking finish:	Butter glaze (optional)

Approximate production time: 3 hours 30 mins
Product life: 2 - 3 days

Mixing Method

- Place all the ingredients except the raisins into a mixing bowl and mix for 20 minutes on slow speed or by hand
- Rest 5 mins and then add the raisins on slow speed or by hand.
- Cover and set aside to ferment in a warm place for 2 hours.
- De-gas after 1 hour

Sancerre

Sancerre is a fine old town, perched on a hill overlooking the valley of the Loire. From the town there are wonderful views of the surrounding hills with terraced vineyards. The whole region is a patchwork quilt of different shades of green stretching for miles across the hills.

Sancerre is a town associated with fine wine and not known for any famous bread varieties to my knowledge. There are one or two bakeries which serve the town and others who concentrate on the tourist trade. The town has spilled out around the base of the hill and this is where the wine industry is to be found.

In Bishop Honoré's day a refuge for the night would have been in a monastic building at the top of the old town. If you should visit Sancerre town do visit the wine museum, an education into wine making and its associated history. In the museum you can sample the town's wine and come away with a souvenir wine glass too. Down the road are the estates that produce La Doucette wines. Other vineyards produce the famous Pouilly Fumé brand.

Château Du Nozet

I have searched for a recipe for bread that would suitably represent Sancerre and the local wine producing region. My friend Gregory came up with a recipe with white wine in it. I have given it the name "Pain Sancerre". The style of cutting the ends of the baguette gives a stylised vine with roots and branches. Artisan bakers do still produce exhibition plaques which feature grapes, grape leaves and vine tendrils arranged on and made with dead dough. This is made with high salt levels to slow or stop fermentation.

More commonly found in shops are hedgehogs and turtles (see "Kid's Stuff").

A château from a distance

Pain Sancerre

Ingredients

Poolish

250g	White bread flour
200g	Water
50g	Wine (red or white)
2g	Yeast fresh

Total 502g

Dough

500g	White bread flour
240g	Water
12g	Yeast fresh
10g	Salt

Total weight: 1.264kg

Dough temp:	38°C
1st speed mix time:	20 mins
1st fermentation time:	1 hour
Conditions:	Ambient, covered
De-gas/knock back:	45 mins
Scale at:	175g
Yield:	7
Resting period:	10 - 15 mins
Tray tin type and size:	38 x 26cm
Warm/prepare:	With oil
Shape and form dough:	Into demi baguettes
Prove at:	25°C
Pre-baking finish:	Cut at moulding
Oven temperature:	230°C (fan 220°C)
Baking time:	12 - 15 mins
Conditions:	With humidity for 10 mins
Post baking finish:	Mist spray exiting the oven

Approximate production time: 2 hours 15 mins
Product life: 1 - 2 days

Mixing Method

- Place the poolish ingredients in a food grade plastic bucket.
- Mix by hand.
- Cover and place in a cool room for 15 - 18 hours.
- Place the dough ingredients in a mixing bowl and add the poolish.
- Mix slowly for 15 - 20 minutes.
- Cover and ferment, de-gas after 45 minutes.
- Scale at 175g for demi baguettes.
- Mould round and rest for 10 minutes.
- Roll out for demi baguettes.
- Place on prepared baking sheets and cut the ends of the baguettes into a "Y" and 3 cuts on the baguette.
  (The Y at each end is a stylised root and branch)

Nevers sur Loire

Nevers is like many of the towns and villages on the river Loire, built on ground well above the highest recorded flood levels so they sit safe and sound. Below the town, vineyards abound on the man made terraces that fringe the river.

In the stone cliffs above the river are caves that once were homes for the local people. No longer inhabited, they have a new use, to store creamy cheese and local wine. The caves are perfect for this purpose because a constant temperature can be guaranteed all year round.

Nevers was a busy port until the 1800s then silt and falling river levels slowed and eventually stopped the port's activities. This town became famous for its fine Persian blue pottery. By the middle ages they were exporting their goods all over France and to many countries in Europe. The town's municipal museum houses some of the finest examples of the potter's art.

Today much of the once un-navigable river has been canalised, allowing commercial and leisure traffic to use the river again. This increased use, as part of the transport network, has breathed new life into riverside towns and villages.

Market stall bread

Fine example of a door

Pain au Lait (Milk Bread) - Viennoiseries

Ingredients

500g	Extra strong bread flour
8g	Salt
50g	Sugar
25g	Milk powder
8g	Malt
15g	Yeast fresh
100g	Butter
230g	Water
60g	Eggs (x 2 - room temperature)

Total 1.86kg

Dough temp:	21°C
Mixing water temp:	_____°C
1st speed mix time:	20 mins
By hand:	20 mins
1st fermentation time:	1 hour 30 mins
Conditions:	Ambient and covered
De-gas/knock back:	45 mins
Scale at:	60g
Yield:	18
Resting period:	10 mins
Tray tin type and size:	38cm x 26cm
Warm/prepare:	Lightly greased with butter
Shape and form dough:	Oval balls, light spray with water, dust with castor sugar and cut
Prove at:	25°C for 45 mins
Pre-baking finish:	At half proof (20 mins) stage cut with scissors like a pine cone
Oven temperature:	190°C (fan 180°C)
Baking time:	8 - 10 mins
Conditions:	With humidity might need heat turned down to 180°C. Take care not to burn the points of the cut dough, cover if necessary.
Post baking finish:	Light dusting with icing sugar is an option, (for children as an afternoon snack, serve with hot chocolate)

Approximate production time: 2 hours 30 mins
Product life: 2 days if you are lucky!

Mixing Method (directe)

- Place the flour, salt, milk powder and butter in the mixing bowl.

- First rub through the butter

- Measure the tepid water and disperse the yeast in it followed by the sugar and eggs.

- Add the liquid phase to the dry ingredients.

- Mix until a smooth extensible dough is achieved.

- Ferment for 90 minutes, covered and put in a warm place.

- De-gas after 45 minutes and cover.

- After 90 minutes scale and mould the dough into balls.

- Rest for 10 minutes.

- Shape into long oval shapes.

- Prove for 45 minutes.

- Mist spray with water and sprinkle with caster sugar.

- Cut after 20 minutes with scissors, looks like a pine cone.

Moulins

The principal town of the Bourbonnais region, naturally it was founded by the Bourbons late in the 11th Century.

When the lands of Brittany and Burgundy became part of France, the independent Bourbons came into conflict with King Françoise. Fearing he would lose his estates to the King, Charles IX, Duke of the Bourbons looked around for allies. Help came from our King Henry VIII who provided mercenaries and cannon.

Rotating windmill

After many battles Charles was killed and King Françoise got his lands and titles. France got a little larger and they named a biscuit in Charles' honour (perhaps). Because of the proximity to the river and the established ecclesiastical buildings, I think our Bishop Honoré might well have had a stopover here on his way south.

Feature fountain

Pain Auvergne (Blue Cheese Bread)

Ingredients

200g	White bread flour
145g	Water (38°C)
4g	Salt
5g	Yeast fresh

Sub total: 354g

300g	White bread flour
60g	Rye flour
220g	Water
2g	Salt
5g	Yeast fresh
354g	Pre-ferment dough
90g	Auvergne blue cheese or Stilton*

Total weight: 1.31kg

Cheese is best chilled

Dough temp:	24°C
Mixing water temp:	_____°C
1st speed mix time:	20 mins (or 20 mins by hand)
1st speed mix time:	20 mins
1st fermentation time:	1 hour
Conditions:	Ambient and covered
De-gas/knock back:	30 mins
Scale at:	500g
Yield:	2
Resting period:	15 mins
Tray tin type and size:	38 x 26cm
Warm/prepare:	Lightly greased
Shape and form dough:	Oval
Prove at:	26°C for 75 mins
Pre-baking finish:	milk wash the dough surface (optional)
Oven temperature:	220°C (fan 210°C)
Baking time:	30 - 35 mins
Conditions:	Humid
Post baking finish:	None

Approximate production time: 3 hours
Product life: 2 - 3 days

Mixing Method

Day 1

- Place in a mixing bowl and mix until a smooth dough has been produced, 5 minutes.
- Put the dough in a plastic container, cover and leave at ambient temperature for 12 - 18 hours.

Day 2

- Place the flours and salt in a mixing bowl.
- Disperse the yeast in tepid water and add to the flour.
- Mix for approximately 10 minutes
- Add the pre-fermented dough and mix for 9 minutes.
- Rest the dough for 10 minutes on the work surface covered.
- Cut the dough into 25cm cubes, dice the cheese into small pieces.
- Distribute the cheese evenly on the dough.
- Draw the dough together and gently reform.
- Cover and ferment for 60 minutes.
- De-gas after 30 minutes. Scale after 60 minutes and form into balls.
- Rest for 10 minutes. Re shape into ovals, place on baking tray.
- Prove for 75 minutes or double in size.

Perfect to eat with Salad

Saint Étienne

The town of Saint Étienne, named after Saint Stephen, stands on the river Fuvan, which in turn feeds into the larger river Loire. Not far from the town the Cistercians founded the Abbey of Valbenoite in 1222. The Abbey was built on a shrine and provided the support needed by pilgrims on their way to Spain. By the 1300s the village had a church; this was dedicated to St Étienne.

They now had a winning medieval combination - on the pilgrim's route, a ford and an ecclesiastical relic or two and your town had arrived. By the late 15th century the village was fortified (a Bastides).

In the 1600s the town had developed an industrial base with coal and steel supporting a newly developed arms industry. The town made swords, bayonets and muskets on an industrial scale. St Étienne was briefly re-named "Arms Town" during the revolution and then was returned to its original name.

With market town status and industry the town grew and prospered. After the arms industry shrank in size it was replaced by the newly formed cycle manufacturing industry.

A local man Paul de Vive was a keen cyclist; he founded the sport of touring on cycles. He edited a cycling magazine and promoted the Derailleur cycle gear - perhaps he had something to do with the Tour de France?

St Étienne is located in the Rhone-Alps region; it has an imposing castle, Rochetaille, and lots of interesting civic buildings. There are several highly respected bakeries in the town and breads can be purchased in the open air market. These are some examples of savoury snacks or food on the move.

Gun Room

Wheat and poppy

Pain aux Olives

Ingredients

250g	White bread flour
250g	Rye flour wholemeal
300g	Levain
20g	Yeast fresh
15g	Salt
450g	Water (38°C)
50g	Black olives (pitted)
50g	Green olives (pitted)

Total 1.385kg

Dough temp:	23°C
Mixing water temp:	_____ °C
1st speed mix time:	4 mins
2nd speed mix time:	12 mins (or 20 mins by hand)
1st fermentation time:	60 - 90 mins
Conditions:	Ambient, moist, covered
De-gas/knock back:	30 - 40 mins
Scale at:	455g
Yield:	3
Resting period:	10 mins
Tray tin type and size:	38 x 26cm
Warm/prepare:	Sheet trays or tile
Shape and form dough:	Bâtard/fougasse
Prove at:	26°C for 60 - 90 mins
Pre-baking finish:	None
Oven temperature:	230°C (fan 220°C) Reduce to 190°C after 25 mins
Baking time:	Bâtard: 45 mins Fougasse: 25 - 30 mins
Conditions:	Humidity for first 12 mins
Post baking finish:	Brush with olive oil immediately on exiting the oven. Cool on wire tray

Approximate production time: 3 hours
Product life: 2 days

Mixing Method

- Place the flours and salt in a bowl.
- Disperse the yeast in the water and add to the flour and salt mixing gently for 4 minutes.
- Add the levain.
- Mix for 20 minutes by hand, or by machine for 12 minutes.
- Rest for 10 minutes.
- Rough cut the dough into cubes.
- Sprinkle the olives onto the dough, (make sure you have drained and pat dried the olives).
- Draw the dough together to incorporate the olives.
- Cover and ferment for 60 -90 minutes.
- De-gas after 40- 60 minutes.
- Scale at 455g and shape into balls.
- Rest for 10 minutes.
- Slightly flatten the ball and shape into a bâtard.
- Cover and prove, or use a rolling pin to roll out the ball of dough into an oval leaf shape.
- Put the dough onto a prepared tray and cut six diagonal slits into the dough, three on each side, then gently open the slits so the dough has the look of a cheese plant.
- Cover and prove.

See also the various types of cuts for an image of fougasse bread. There is a photo of a cut fougasse on the recipe page for Paris. The cuts aid speedy baking.

Cheese, chorizo & black olives

Valence

Valence, known in Roman times as Valentia Julia, was recognised as a city with strategic trade routes in all directions. The Romans lost this vital city in the 5th century to various groups of barbarians, who also recognised this city's strengths. Then came the Frankish/Arab and even German interest and influences.

With the support of the Pope in Avignon, the Bishops of Valence joined with Die to form a large and influential Bishopric. From Valence, Bishop Honoré might have stayed within the bishopric and travelled to Crest in the Drôme valley.

Valence has prospered by its location. It sits like Lyon on the ancient North-South trade route from the Mediterranean port of Marseille. Pilgrims and traders passed through, stayed, bought and sold, and the town prospered.

Modern day Valence is a transport hub, with a port on the river Rhone, a railway and airport facilities. Most importantly it still sits on the north-south road links, with branches to Grenoble and on to Geneva. The Romans clearly knew a thing a two about transport and locations. Valence has its market, bakers and too many supermarket outlets for bread.

Young baker at work

Trio of poppies

1000 year old dog's paw print

Le Pain Scie

Ingredients

Poolish

125g	White bread flour
125g	Water
2g	Yeast fresh

Total 252g

325g	White bread flour
50g	Rye flour
185g	Water
5g	Yeast fresh
7g	Salt

Total weight: 824g

Dough temp:	28°C
Mixing water temp:	_____°C
1st speed mix time:	7 mins
2nd speed mix time:	10 mins (or 17 mins by hand)
1st fermentation time:	70 mins
Conditions:	Ambient and covered
De-gas/knock back:	40 mins
Scale at:	410g strip x 2
Yield:	2
Resting period:	10 mins
Tray tin type and size:	38 x 26cm
Warm/prepare:	Lightly greased
Shape and form dough:	See diagram
Prove at:	23°C for 60 mins
Pre-baking finish:	dust with flour, cut and place in an arc
Oven temperature:	240°C (fan 230°C)
Baking time:	18 mins
Conditions:	With humidity for 10 mins
Post baking finish:	None

Approximate production time: 5 hours
Product life: 1 day

Mixing Method (fabrication sur poolish)

- Mix the first stage and place in a container with space to expand and cover for 3 hours at 25°C
- Mix all the ingredients including the poolish (except the salt).
- Mix for 7 minutes on slow, or by hand.
- Add a teaspoon of boiling water to the salt to soften it.
- Then add the salt to the dough and mix for a further 10 minutes on slow speed, or by hand.
- Cover and ferment for 70 minutes.
- De-gas after 40 minutes.
- Cover and complete the ferment.
- Scale, shape and cut (see diagram)

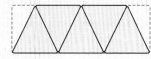

- Dust with flour and form the triangles into 2 arcs with points of all the triangles pointing upwards like the sharks teeth. Then form into an arc.

Crest

Crest is an attractive market town with its own peculiar road system which I imagine must be due to the ancient street plan. The town grew up around the castle that dominates the valley. The fortification, being at the head of the valley, would be able to observe tax and control all travellers coming up the valley from Die (pronounced *Dee*).

Market days are a joy, with lots of produce supplied by local small holders. Because much of the fruit and vegetables are locally grown, the quality is superb. The town's bakers are still thriving and one clearly supplies the stall on the market. The ancient town sat astride the East-West trade route between Die and Valence. Bishop Honoré might have preached here if he had taken a bed in the castle.

Pain au son ready for the oven

Bridge at Crest and the castle

Pain au Son (Bran Bread)

Ingredients

125g	Bran
360g	Water (38°C)
300g	White bread flour T55
75g	Rye flour
10g	Salt
10g	Yeast fresh
5g	Milk powder
125g	Pre-ferment dough

Total 1.1kg

Dough temp:	25°C
Mixing water temp:	_____°C
1st speed mix time:	3 mins
2nd speed mix time:	12 mins (or 20 mins by hand)
1st fermentation time:	40 mins
Conditions:	Ambient and covered
De-gas/knock back:	40 mins
Scale at:	250g
Yield:	4
Resting period:	20 mins
Tray tin type and size:	38 x 26cm
Warm/prepare:	Lightly greased
Shape and form dough:	Roll out the dough into an oblong and cut into 4 triangles. Place on the tray
Prove at:	24°C for 1 hour
Pre-baking finish:	Spray with water and sprinkle with bran on top
Oven temperature:	230°C (fan 210°C)
Baking time:	20 - 25mins
Conditions:	No steam required
Post baking finish:	None

Approximate production time: 4 hours
Product life: 2 days

Mixing method

- Place the bran and 250g of water at 38°C in a bowl and stand for 30 minutes.
- Add the rye, bread flour, milk powder and water and mix slowly for 3 minutes, or by hand
- Let the mixture stand for 15 minutes.
- Add the salt, then the yeast in a little water.
- Mix vigorously by hand or 2 speed on a machine for 6 minutes.
- Add the pre-fermented dough and mix for a further 6 minutes.
- Place the dough in a bowl, cover and ferment for 40 minutes.
- De-gas after 20 minutes and then ferment for a further 20 minutes.
- Divide the dough into two.
- Roll each half into an oblong about 26cm by 15cm, and then cut into four or five triangles.
- Spray with water, sprinkle with bran and place on a greased tray about 2cm apart.
- Leave to prove for an hour then bake.

Vercheny

The village of Vercheny is located midway between Crest at the top of the valley and Die at the bottom. There has been a bakery in Vercheny since the 1900s.

There were once similar bakeries in the surrounding villages and hamlets in the hills and up and down the valley but most of these have lost their bakeries because their former customers now drive to Die or Valence to do their shopping in the supermarkets.

So Krystal runs the baker's shop in Vercheny and her husband makes and bakes the bread in the old way. Grandfather delivers to the local hamlets and helps out. The shop window and display are stacked with the night's work. Pain a l'Ancienne, bâtard aux cereals and pain complete sit in baskets ready for delivery. Flutes, boules and le tordu are stacked on the counter ready to be delivered.

Mountains above the Drôme

The bulk of the breads produced are rustic in nature with blends of flour types and lots of seeds and grains included. The bread that best represents this bakery and the valley is *Pain de la Drôme*.

Shop at Vercheny

Crusty breads from the shop at Vercheny

Pain de la Drôme

Ingredients

400g	Wholemeal bread flour
100g	Light rye flour
10g	Salt
100g	Pre-fermented dough
10g	Yeast fresh
20g	Brown or golden linseed
310g	Water

Total 950g

Dough temp:	26°C
Mixing water temp:	_____°C
1st speed mix time:	15 mins
1st fermentation time:	1 hour
Conditions:	Warm and covered
De-gas/knock back:	45 mins
Scale at:	300g
Yield:	3+
Resting period:	10 mins
Tray tin type and size:	38 x 26cm tile or tray
Warm/prepare:	Coarse rice flour
Shape and form dough:	See diagram
Prove at:	23°C for 1 hour
Pre-baking finish:	Mist spray & sprinkle with golden linseeds
Oven temperature:	220°C (fan 210°C)
Baking time:	25 mins
Conditions:	with humidity for 20 mins
Post baking finish:	Mist spray immediately on exiting the oven. Cooling on wire trays

Approximate production time: 2 hours 15 mins
Product life: 1 - 2 days

Mixing Method

- Place all but the pre-fermented dough in the bowl.
- Add the yeast which has been dispersed in the water, mix for 5 minutes slowly.
- Cover for 30 minutes.
- Add the pre-fermented dough and mix for 10 minutes on slow speed or by hand.
- Cover and ferment for 60 minutes.
- De-gas after 45 minutes.
- Scale and mould round.
- Rest for 10 minutes.
- Cut with a kitchen knife as indicated in the diagram.:

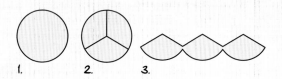

The bread shape represents the mountains along the valley of the Drôme

75

Die

(Pronounced *Dee* by the locals)

Ancient Die was developed by the Romans who fortified the town and used it as an administrative centre for the lower Drôme valley.

The first formal records of Christianity are of Bishop Martinus AD 220, the first Bishop of Die. Bishop Nicasius appears to have attended the First Council of Nicaea AD 325. Also Bishop Lucretius AD 541- 573 (famed for being a miracle worker) might well have welcomed our Bishop Honoré on his pilgrimage through the Drôme valley to Avignon.

To travel to Avignon, Honoré would have left via the Roman gate that stands at the south side of the town. He would have travelled by road at this stage, as the Drôme is not navigable after Die unless you are into extreme sports, like white water rafting and canoeing. My first view of the Drôme at Die was from the mountains, looking just like a sapphire blue snake travelling along the valley bottom.

On route, Bishop Honoré would have passed a place called Pic de Luc. It was here, long after Honoré's time, when one of those incredible acts of nature took place. In the year AD 1442 one whole side of the mountain collapsed. This caused slabs of rock as big as a double decker bus to be carried down the mountain side; this effectively cut the Drôme valley off from the South of France.

This area is now known as the "Claps de Lucen Diois" a paradise for rock climbers and canoeists; they say it's an ill wind. A route through this pile of great rocks was established in the 1800s which is not for the faint hearted or those with a fear of heights (like me). This route is an oversized goat track, but will give the traveller some memorable views from the top. Modern pilgrims, in the 1920s, the moneyed set, would go on safari through the mountains. Driving early motor cars they stayed at remote roadside inns on their way to St Tropez and Monte Carlo.

The view from the top of the mountains is worth the effort of getting there. It was at about this time I noticed the change in vegetation and the construction of the buildings. On the north side of the Alps, buildings and trees appeared to cling to the mountain side, perhaps braced as if they expected to be swept away by an avalanche. To the south the trees look more relaxed and houses are less "Alpine" in construction. The feeling is one of a fertile plain stretching out on either side of the Route Napoleon.

Bakers in this part of France often bake on coarse ground olive stones, this avoids scorching the bread base. Baking on ground olive stones imparts a subtle and yet distinctive flavour to the breads of the Mediterranean.

River Drôme

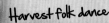

Harvest folk dance

Claps de Lucen Diois

Pogne de Romans

Ingredients

500g	Bread flour
50g	Milk (38°C)
30g	Yeast fresh
7g	Salt
50g	Sugar
200g	Pre-fermented dough
275g	Eggs (38°C)
5g	Orange flower water
140g	Butter (room temperature)
12g	Orange zest (2 oranges)
5g	Orange liquor

Total 1.274kg

Dough temp:	23°C
Mixing water temp:	_____°C
1st speed mix time:	20 mins
2nd speed mix time:	5 mins
1st fermentation time:	2 hours
Conditions:	Warm and covered
De-gas/knock back:	1 hour
Scale at:	630g
Resting period:	10 mins
Tray tin type and size:	Large brioche or place on a prepared tray
Shape and form dough:	Rounds with central hole
Prove at:	25°C for 3 hours (or twice the size)
Pre-baking finish:	Whole egg wash, sprinkle with broken cube sugar or coffee crystals
Oven temperature:	190°C (fan 180°C)
Baking time:	40 mins
Conditions:	Bake with humidity
Post baking finish:	Orange sugar glaze

Approximate production time: 4 hours
Product life: 5 days

Mixing Method

- Disperse the yeast in the milk. Add the warm eggs and milk to the dry ingredients, also the orange flower water.

- Mix on a slow speed and produce a well developed dough, approximately 20 minutes mixing.

- Add the butter and mix to produce smooth silky dough, approximately 5 minutes on 2nd speed.

- Cover and ferment for 1 hour in a warm place.

- Return to the mixer.

- Add the zest of 2 medium oranges and 1 tablespoon of orange liquor, e.g. Triple Sec, or Grand Marnier.

- Ferment for further 1 hour.

Trigance

In the Region Natural du Verdon

This town is literally fused to the sides of the canyon; houses closest to the canyon side are cut into the rock. I suppose they could be described as caves with house fronts. On the other side of the street, houses hang like limpets, on foundations cut into steps on the outer edge of the hill. These homes are hundreds of years old and will be there when many modern dwellings have fallen down. Here, houses remain cool in the heat of summer and yet are easy to heat in winter.

At the very top of the hill sits the château which has unrestricted views of the valleys on either side. If you follow the road up the hill you come to the village square, "Le Place Honoré Giraud", named in honour of a famous General, who served France in both the world wars. On the place stands the shop belonging to our friends Monique and Patrick Bastiani. Patrick makes and bakes the breads, brioches, pissaladieres and naviettes (biscuits), transporting them up the hill to the shop. His bakery has been in the family for two generations now and as I write, Patrick's son is in the process of taking over from his father, making it three generations.

The bakery is a separate building from Patrick's home and shop, a common practice because of the fire risk. The bakery operates on a very old system called pour banal, which means the village owns the bakery oven and the villagers could, if they so wished, use it. In the 1800s the ladies of the village would have put their pot roasts and bread in the oven using it on a daily basis with the agreement of the baker. All that was required was a contribution, a little wood or some small coins.

Patrick's oven

The oven is a Roman type (like an igloo in stone) heated by a fire of wood. The wood for the oven is stored at the bottom of the hill and Patrick brings enough wood up each day for the firing of the oven. Fires are lit at 11pm and when the flames have died down, the ashes are raked out and the oven sole is brushed clean. Then the oven is ready to receive the first batches of rolls for baking.

The oven operates on the principle of small breads and rolls first, the oven being at its hottest. As the oven cools down, larger breads are baked, followed by brioches, cakes, biscuits and then perhaps chickens and hams. The oven rarely cools right down, the latent heat remains for days. I think this is the oldest working oven in France. Monique runs her shop and supplies the village and hundreds of tourists who walk up the hill, (no traffic in this medieval town) with bread and cakes and the best pissaladiere I have ever tasted.

Patrick and Monique

The oven by night

La Pissaladiere

Ingredients

Pizza dough

500g	Bread flour
15g	Baking powder
10g	Herbs de Provence
125g	Olive oil
15g	Salt
5g	Ground black pepper
10g	Milk powder
30g	Egg
225g	Water
15g	Yeast fresh
5g	Sugar

Total 955g

Dough temp:	21°C
Mixing water temp:	_____°C
1st speed mix time:	15 mins
1st fermentation time:	90 mins
Conditions:	Warm and covered
De-gas/knock back:	45 mins
Scale at:	240g
Yield:	4
Resting period:	15 mins
Tray tin type and size:	38 x 26cm or tile
Warm/prepare:	Baking parchment
Shape and form dough:	Roll out and prick with a fork
Prove at:	25°C for 30 mins
Pre-baking finish:	See notes
Oven temperature:	220°C (fan 210°C)
Baking time:	20 mins
Conditions:	Dry bake
Post baking finish:	See notes

Approximate production time: 2 hours 30 mins
Product life: 2 days (stored at 3°C)

Mixing Method

- Mix the ingredients together to produce smooth elastic dough.
- Cover and set aside for 90 minutes.
- Divide into 4 roll out onto a sheet of oven parchment approximately 38cm x 26cm or to fit your oven tile.
- Place the pizza on a stiff sheet of corrugated paper (side of a box).
- Apply the topping.
- Give a final proof of 30 minutes.
- Use the corrugated sheet to aid transfer onto a pre-heated oven tile in the oven. *(NB: wear gloves)*

Topping

- Select 6 medium sized onions and cut thinly, fry in olive oil until they are just starting to brown.
- Cool and spread over the surface of the dough.
- Decorate the tops of the onions with strips of anchovies or sardines in oil (you may need to cut these length ways as they are large fish). The fish should form a decorative lattice pattern.
- Put half of a small black olive in the centre of each diamond.
- Cover and stand for 30 minutes, or keep in fridge until required. Bake at 220°C (fan 210°C). The dough at the edges should be chestnut brown.
- Cool slightly then remove from the baking tray to avoid the base sweating. Decorate with basil leaves or drizzle basil infused oil over surface. Eat hot or cold with salad or as a fridge snack.

Avignon

Pont St-Benezet

So in 1309 Pope Clement V moved to Avignon, and the city became the capital of Christianity. 1310 found Pope Clement accepting the dissolution of the Order of the Knights Templar. There have been a few historic novels written on that subject. With all of the Papal influences the city was architecturally transformed by many beautiful buildings which were commissioned and built. Avignon stands on the Rhone and this is a possible route by which Bishop Honoré might have visited the city.

Port Saint Benezet was begun, according to folklore and legend, in 1177 by a shepherd boy called Benezet, who was to be the founder of the "Bridge Brotherhood" (I know I keep going on about bridges and fords being the key to the continued prosperity of a town or city). The Brotherhood built the Saint Esprit Bridge over a hundred years later. This was no mean feat of engineering and was the only stone bridge over the mighty river Rhone. In the 17th century, flood waters carried away 18 of the bridge's arches. Alas no more dancing across the bridge at Avignon (*P.S. they do still dance on the bridge at least once a year*). The city is famous for arts and culture and naturally for its bread and pastries.

Avignon! For me this was a place remembered from a childhood nursery rhyme. Here happy people danced on the bridge, I knew not why but I knew the rhyme by heart, and in French. I feel sure that was the case for many children of the 40s along with Brother Jack and the bells of morning. So here I was at Avignon looking at the river and wondering about the history of this place so far away from my home in Yorkshire.

Avignon was for many years the residence of the Pope, in fact the first seven Popes here were French. The last Pope of Avignon was Gregory XI who was one of three non French Popes who ruled from Avignon. In 1377 Pope Gregory departed for Rome leaving the Papal legates to administer in Avignon until 1791. Avignon was a retreat from the high politics of Rome and was part of the Papal territories up to it being re-united with France in 1791.

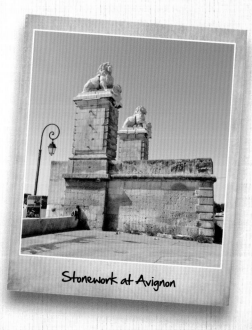

Stonework at Avignon

A Holy Relic

Pain de Mie

Ingredients

1kg	White bread flour
650g	Water or milk
40g	Yeast fresh
16g	Salt
50g	Sugar
40g	Milk powder
100g	Butter

Total 1.896kg

Dough temp:	24°C
Mixing water temp:	_____ °C
Mixing time:	20 mins by hand
1st fermentation time:	1 hour
Conditions:	Ambient and covered
De-gas/knock back:	40 mins
Scale at:	550g - 600g, depending on the size of the tin
Yield:	3
Resting period:	10 mins
Tray tin type and size:	Long loaf tin
Warm/prepare:	Lightly greased
Shape and form dough:	Bâtard
Prove at:	26°C for 30 mins
Pre-baking finish:	None
Oven temperature:	220°C (fan 210°C)
Baking time:	25 - 30 mins
Conditions:	Humid
Post baking finish:	None

Approximate production time: 3 hours
Product life: 4 days

Mixing Method

- Place the flour, milk powder, yeast and butter in a bowl.
- Dissolve the sugar in the water (tepid) and add to the above.
- Mix for 10 minutes on slow speed.
- Add the salt dissolved in 5g of hot water to the mixture and mix for a further 10 minutes.
- Cover and ferment for 60 - 80 minutes.
- De-gas after 30 minutes
- Scale and shape, place the dough into prepared tins and prove to an internal height of 75% of the volume of the tin.
- Put the 3 tins with the dough in on a baking tray.
- Take a similar tray to put over the 3 loaf tins. If the tray's edge prevents the complete sealing of the loaf tins, use the underside of the tray, prepared with grease.
- You should at this stage have the three tins sandwiched between the two trays. Now you need a heavy object to keep the top tray from lifting up. Cast iron cookware or weight from your scales or even a couple of new house bricks will do to hold it down.
- Bake for 20 minutes, then with great care remove the weight, lift and remove the top tray and finish baking.

Arles

I was keen to see the Roman amphitheatre at Arles. I guess attending a part time course on Roman archaeology had kindled my enthusiasm. After parking we walked to the amphitheatre to be greeted by swallows darting through the sunlit arched galleries. The place is very old and every corner you turn there is something ancient to look at and it just exudes history.

Arles was first colonised by the Greeks in the 6th century BC and then predictably by the Romans on their way up the conquests league table. As the Roman Empire expanded, Arles played an ever increasing important role in the Roman supply/logistics system, transport links being further improved by the canal from Arles to the sea. No shortage of labour in those days, as slaves and prisoners were on hand to dig it.

Arles was selected by Caesar to be a veteran's colony; Roman soldiers who had served their time would receive land and could take a wife, settle down and join the community. Romans built ships for warfare in the estuary. They eventually left, but their skills remained and boat building continued. Arles became an important maritime facility, it was closer to the sea in those days and now perhaps due to falling sea levels it's an inland town. Out of the port, in a northerly direction ran the ever straight Roman highway, sadly now long gone. This road would link up with the East-West routes at Valence going to the Atlantic coast or the troops in Germania.

Artists still come to Arles for the Mediterranean light and the wealth of subject matter. Vincent van Gogh painted his now famous Sunflowers and other canvases in and around the town. The Romans liked to keep their citizens happy with bread and circuses. The bread was a flour allowance, probably Spelt, and the circuses,

The Roman amphitheatre

gladiators, chariot races and exotic birds and animals from the corners of the Empire.

I have chosen Mediterranean country bread, with rye, spelt and sunflower seeds. Like the Roman soldier this is solid, dependable bread that can be eaten with your picnic.

Modern day Arles is an important administrative centre and has some of the best bakers in the region. There are splendid museums, art galleries, Roman ruins and artefacts.

Another view of the amphitheatre

Pain aux Graines de Tournesol

Ingredients

400g	Wholemeal bread flour
50g	Rye flour
50g	Spelt flour
10g	Yeast fresh
100g	Pre-fermented dough
15g	Sunflower oil
60g	Toasted sunflower seeds
30g	Toasted sesame seeds
325g	Water
20g	Sesame seeds (non toasted)

Total 1.6kg

Dough temp:	22°C
Mixing water temp:	_____°C
1st speed mix time:	8 mins
2nd speed mix time:	12 mins
1st fermentation time:	2 hours
Conditions:	Ambient and covered
De-gas/knock back:	1 hour
Scale at:	500g
Yield:	2
Resting period:	10 mins
Tray tin type and size:	38 x 26cm
Warm/prepare:	Warm and greased
Shape and form dough:	Boules
Prove at:	25°C for 40 - 60 mins
Pre-baking finish:	Spray with water & sprinkle with sesame seeds, cut the top with scissors to form a cross
Oven temperature:	220°C (fan 210°C)
Baking time:	35 - 40 mins
Conditions:	With humidity for 25 mins *NB: Turn the oven down if the seeds start to become too brown*
Post baking finish:	None

Approximate production time: 3 hours 30 mins
Product life: 3 days

Mixing Method

- Mix the flour, yeast, water and oil together for 6 minutes to form dough.
- Add the salt and 5g of hot water taken from the recipe.
- Mix for a further 2 minutes.
- Continue mixing for 10 minutes on 2nd speed or by hand.
- Add the toasted seeds and mix until the seeds are fully incorporated into the dough.
- Cover and ferment for 2 hours.
- De-gas after 1 hour and cover.
- Scale and shape roughly into boules.
- Rest for 10 minutes.
- Mould again into boules
- Prove for 40 - 60 minutes.
- Spray with water and sprinkle with non toasted sesame seeds.

Nîmes

Nîmes like Arles, boasts some fine Roman buildings. The Arena built in the reign of Augustus pre-dates the one in Arles and is definitely worth a visit. Nîmes is a wonderful place with parks and gardens, some with water features to cool the hot and weary traveller.

The blue pottery and famous blue cloth get their inspiration from the blue summer skies of the Mediterranean. Levi Strauss used this colour for his renowned work wear in America. The term "de Nîmes" corrupted slightly to become denim and this became a multimillion dollar industry.

The Artisan breads of the Mediterranean become flatter and because of the influence of the ground olive stones they are baked on, appear to have a nicer taste. One of the brioche varieties we found locally was that of Saint Genix. This is a striking variety of brioche because of its raspberry red almond pralines. If you see them on your travels in France buy a box of them so you can make this delicious brioche at home.

Pralines St Genix

The road to Nîmes

Bridge over the Rhone

84

Pain Saint Genix (Brioche)

Ingredients

250g	Strong white bread flour
20g	Milk (38°C)
15g	Yeast fresh
5g	Salt
25g	Sugar
135g	Eggs (38°C)
2g	Orange flower water
2g	Rum
5g	Zest and juice ½ lemon
70g	Butter
100g	Pre-fermented dough
200g	Pralines aux Amandes

Total 829g

Dough temp:	24°C
Mixing water temp:	_____°C
1st speed mix time:	20 mins
1st fermentation time:	2 hours
Conditions:	Covered and warm
De-gas/knock back:	1 hour (+ ferment 1 hour)
Scale at:	410g
Yield:	2
Resting period:	10 mins
Tray tin type and size:	Silicone sheet or well greased tray
Shape and form dough:	Into a dome shape
Prove at:	25°C for 1 hour (or until double in size)
Pre-baking finish:	Egg and milk wash then snip with scissors
Oven temperature:	180°C (Reduce to 165°C)
Baking time:	20 - 25 mins
Conditions:	Coolish oven required, mid shelf. Cover if too much colour is taken
Post baking finish:	After cooling lightly dust with icing sugar or dextrose. Or 50:50 syrup and orange liquor on exiting the oven

Approximate production time: 5 hours
Product life: 2 - 3 days

Mixing Method

- Place the flour and salt in a bowl.
- Put the warm milk, eggs, yeast and juices together in a bowl and add the yeast, mix lightly and add to the flour.
- Mix this for 5 minutes on slow and form dough.
- Add the butter and mix for a further 5 minutes on slow speed.
- Mix in the pre-fermented dough and mix for 5 minutes on slow.
- Place in a bowl and cover for 60 minutes.
- After 60 minutes de-gas, and return to the bowl. Cover for a further 60 minutes. Finally de-gas and rest for 10 minutes.
- Cut the dough into cubes, add the pralines and draw the dough together making sure the pralines are distributed evenly. Divide the dough into 2 and shape into balls.
- Slightly flatten into a dome shape.
- Place on a warm tray and prove.

Narbonne

Narbonne is a Mediterranean city and has a history that goes back to the 7th century BC. It was founded as a Gallic settlement on the high ground north of the city after Hannibal was defeated. The Romans had started their expansion through the Mediterranean and needed a port based on the French side of the water. Narbonne was chosen to be the senatorial colony and Rome's link with Spain over land and as part of the Roman's commercial and military hub this brought wealth and expansion. An artificial port was created by diverting part of the river Aude. Narbonne was made capital of Gallia Narbonensis and remained a jewel in the Roman crown till the end of the Empire. A succession of invasions affected the city, first came Visigoths, who made it their capital. Muslim raiders came over land from Spain and looted the city and then left.

Fortified home

Narbonne was firmly on the pilgrim's route and its link to Spain, and was a popular port at the time of Bishop Honoré. It was used to navigate the coastal regions of the Mediterranean. In the 14th century a huge storm swept away the Roman water link to the port. The change in the river and tidal flow caused the old port to silt up and the port's trade went into steep decline. In the early 1800s the Canal du Midi was built along with the Suez, and this changed the fortunes of the city. The railways added further to its return to prosperity.

Bakers are many and the influences are also very Mediterranean.

Fortified homes

Pain Naranja (Orange Bread)

Ingredients

Section A

330g	Bread flour
65g	Water
6g	Salt
65g	Masa madre*
35g	Yeast fresh

Section B

20g	Butter
1g	Anise powder
65g	Orange zest and juice
50g	Egg (1 small)
35g	Sunflower oil
55g	Granulated sugar

Total 727g

Masa madre (pre-fermented dough)

Dough temp:	27°C
Mixing water temp:	_____°C
1st speed mix time:	15 - 20 mins
1st fermentation time:	15 mins
Conditions:	Warm and covered
De-gas/knock back:	None
Scale at:	360g
Yield:	2
Resting period:	10 mins
Tray tin type and size:	38 x 26cm
Shape and form dough:	Into two balls, slightly flattened
Prove at:	25°C for 1 hour 15 mins
Pre-baking finish:	Egg wash lightly and roll in granulated sugar
Oven temperature:	180°C (fan 170°C)
Baking time:	25 - 30 mins
Conditions:	With steam, tray of water in base of the oven
Post baking finish:	None, or for luxury version brush with orange liquor

Approximate production time: 3 hours 30 mins
Product life: 5 days

Mixing Method

- Place the ingredients of section **A** in a mixing bowl.
- Mix to form a rough dough, 1 minute.
- **B** Zest and juice of a medium orange made up to 65g, with extra orange juice if required.
- Place the 65g of orange, sugar, oil, butter and anise powder in a jug.
- Mix for a moment and pour into the mixing bowl with ingredients **A**
- Mix gently by hand for 15 - 20 minutes.
- Place the dough in a bowl and cover for 15 minutes.
- Remove and scale into 2 x 36g.
- Mould roughly round, rest for 10 minutes, then mould round again.
- Lightly wash with egg and milk mixture.
- Roll into granulated sugar.
- Place onto a prepared baking sheet and prove.

Production note

Take care not to burn the top of the bread.

Carcassonne

This is a fortified town that looks like a Hollywood backdrop, but it is not what it appears. This site has been fought over, lost, destroyed and rebuilt many times since it was first founded by the Romans. The walled town of Carcassonne was an important stronghold for the Cathars, a controversial religious sect who had rejected much of the Christian teachings. The Cathars avant-garde approach to worship clearly angered the Pope. After some deliberation and arm twisting, he secured an army and launched his crusade. The army's brief was to stamp out the religious practices of the Cathars. No exceptions would be made - low borne or noble birth, a death warrant had been signed for the Cathars.

Not a great deal is actually known about the Cathars, as most of their religious texts were destroyed by the Catholic Crusaders, but they appeared to have enjoyed the popularity afforded the Jews in Nazi Germany.

The nearby town of Beziers was attacked first and the inhabitants, both Catholics and Cathars, appear to have fought side by side against the Crusaders. When the town was taken, it was decreed that the townspeople where to be massacred as an example to everyone. A Cistercian abbot–commander was asked prior to the killing, "How we can tell the Cathars from the Catholics?". His reply was "Kill them all, the Lord will recognise his own". Reportedly more than seven thousand people died, many more than the town might have normally held as sadly many people who lived outside of the town had fled there for safety.

Carcassonne

Carcassonne itself was then put to siege and after a couple of weeks and the loss of their chief representative Raymond-Roger Trencavel, who was captured by deceit after being invited to parley, the demoralised inhabitants of the town ran out of water and it was all over. Trencavel died age 24 years in his own prison under suspicious circumstances, leaving a young son, Raymond the Second, who some years later attempted to take the castle and his inheritance back by force. Aided by the townsfolk, he attacked Carcassonne in 1240 but failed to take the fort as it was held by a superior force led by Simon de Montfort. Louis IX had the fortifications razed to the ground to make sure that there could be no more Cathar uprisings. In 1853 the ruins of the castle were restored and the castle of Carcassonne took on the medieval look it has today. It is now listed as a World Heritage site and has lots of activities for all ages, including far too many shops.

The bread for Carcassonne, the pain boule, resembles the stones used in the siege, examples of which can be seen in the castle today.

The walls of Carcassonne

Carcassonne from the river

Pain Boule

Ingredients

Poolish

125g	White bread flour
125g	Water (38°C)
3g	Yeast fresh

Sub total 253g

62g	Rye flour
440g	White bread flour
320g	Water
4g	Yeast fresh
10g	Salt

Total weight: 1.89kg

Poolish temp:	28°C
Dough temp:	25°C
Mixing water temp:	_____°C
1st speed mix time:	5 mins
2nd speed mix time:	10 mins (or 18 mins by hand)
1st fermentation time:	90 mins
Conditions:	Ambient and covered
De-gas/knock back:	45 mins
Scale at:	500g
Yield:	2
Resting period:	10 mins
Tray tin type and size:	Tile or 38 x 26cm tray
Shape and form dough:	Into a round ball
Prove at:	25°C for 45 mins
Pre-baking finish:	Flour and cut and place immediately in the oven
Oven temperature:	230°C (fan 220°C)
Baking time:	20 - 35 mins
Conditions:	With a water bath in base of the oven (humidity)
Post baking finish:	None

Approximate production time: 5 hours
Product life: 2 days

Mixing Method

- Mix poolish, cover and set aside in a warm place for 90 minutes.
- Place the rye, wheat flour and salt in the mixing bowl.
- Disperse the yeast in tepid water.
- Add the water and the poolish to the mixing bowl.
- Mix slowly for 5 minutes to form basic dough (adjust the consistency if necessary), then further mix for 10 minutes to produce smooth extensible dough.
- Place in a bowl and cover to ferment for 90 minutes.
- De-gas after 45 minutes.
- After 90 minutes de-gas and scale 2 x 500g units.
- Mould roughly round.
- Rest for 10 minutes.
- Mould into boules.
- Place upside down in two cloth lined bowls; prepared with flour, twice the size of the boule (expansion room).
- After 45 minutes turn out onto a baking tray or tile.
- Flour and cut.
- Place in the oven immediately.

Pau

This is the end of the French territory; the town of Pau has guarded the entrance to the Somport Pass since the Romans had built an earth and wooden fort there. There are plenty of fortifications in the area as this would be an ideal route for invaders from the south. The pass would take our pilgrims on their way into Spain and their goal of a visit to the holy relics at Santiago de Compostela.

Perhaps the bread for Pau should reflect the Spanish influences in the town; this is Castillo Blanco, white castellated bread from Spain.

As we travelled back from Spain through the Somport Pass the sun was setting. Rose coloured light played on the long abandoned fortress, guarding the pass. This was like a scene from one of the Dracula films. As the last rays of the sun squeezed between the rocks, I thought of garlic bread, steaks and a comfortable bed for the night. We got a Formula One in Pau and a pizza instead.

Château-et-soleil

Steps of the château

Fortified watch tower

Pilgrims route

Pain Castillo Blanco

Ingredients

400g	White bread flour
7g	Salt
15g	Yeast fresh
100g	Malted flour
305g	Water
10g	Butter
150g	Pre-fermented dough

Total 987g

Mixing Method (straight dough)

- Disperse the yeast in the water, and then add it to the other ingredients.
- Mix on slow speed or by hand for 20 minutes.
- Cover the dough and set aside for 60 minutes in a warm place.
- De-gas after 40 minutes and cover.
- Scale at 490g. Rest for 10 minutes.
- Roll out into a disc.
- Prove for 60 - 70 minutes.
- Dust with rye flour and cut.

Dough temp:	21°C
Mixing water temp:	_____°C
Mixing time:	20 mins
1st fermentation time:	1 hour
Conditions:	Ambient and covered
De-gas/knock back:	40 mins
Scale at:	490g
Yield:	2
Resting period:	10 mins
Tray tin type and size:	Sheet, tray or tile
Warm/prepare:	Dust with semolina flour
Shape and form dough:	Into balls, rest, then flatten with a rolling pin
Prove at:	23°C for 60 - 70 mins
Pre-baking finish:	Flour and cut (see diagram)
Oven temperature:	220°C (fan 210°C)
Baking time:	40 mins
Conditions:	With humidity for 30mins
Post baking finish:	None

Approximate production time: 2 hours
Product life: 2 days

Toulouse

The early city of Toulouse was the capital of the Visigothic Kingdom. Christianity traces its early foundation to the church of Saint Pierre Cusines. This church has a 4th century crypt, with its church being rebuilt in the 11th and 12th century. Firmly astride the major trade routes between the Atlantic sea and the Mediterranean the city prospered.

Pilgrims used this city as it was on the routes of Santiago de Compostela. The Basilica of St Sermin being a place to stay on the pilgrimage for bread and bed. The Church of the Jacobins is the burial place of Saint Thomas Aquinas. By the Middle Ages Toulouse had become one of the main French centres of culture and artistic activity. With Royal patronage the city grew and prospered.

Modern Toulouse is a vibrant city with Airbus France having its Head Quarters in the city. Photographers please note, the Galerie du Château d'Eau is thought to be one of the oldest places dedicated to photography - smile! Toulouse in my view is Rugby Union and sausages. Stand Toulousain is Toulouse's famous rugby club. Saucisse de Toulouse is the sausage and pain au saucisson is my choice of bread to represent the city.

Slices of pain au saucisson

Pain au Saucisson

Ingredients

450g	White bread flour
50g	Rye bread flour
15g	Yeast fresh
8g	Salt
125g	Sausage (quality pork)
10g	Basil infused olive oil
5g	Black treacle
270g	Water
150g	Pre-fermented dough (min 12 hours)

Total 1.83kg

Dough temp:	25°C
Mixing water temp:	_____°C
1st speed mix time:	6 mins + 2 mins
2nd speed mix time:	10 mins (or 20 mins by hand)
1st fermentation time:	1 hour
Conditions:	Cover (damp cloth)
De-gas/knock back:	30 mins
Scale at:	360g
Yield:	3
Resting period:	10 mins
Tray tin type and size:	38 x 26cm
Warm/prepare:	Lightly greased
Shape and form dough:	Into bâtards
Prove at:	27°C for 1 hour
Pre-baking finish:	Lightly flour and cut (or see post baking options)
Oven temperature:	230°C (fan 220°C)
Baking time:	25 mins
Conditions:	With moisture for 75% of the bake
Post baking finish:	Brush hot with chilli and garlic pizza oil (optional)

Approximate production time: 3 hours
Product life: 2 days

Mixing Method

- Fry the sausage for 10 minutes on a low heat.
- Drain and cool, cut them into 1cm slices.
- Place the flours, yeast and salt in a bowl.
- Put the treacle, oil and tepid water in a jug and dissolve the treacle.
- Add the liquid to the flour.
- Mix to form an elastic dough on slow mix for 6 minutes.
- Add the pre-fermented dough and mix for 10 minutes.
- Rest the dough for 10 minutes.
- Add the cooked and cooled sausage, mix for 2 minutes slow.
- Cover and ferment for 60 minutes.
- De-gas after 30 minutes.
- After 60 minutes scale and mould roughly into balls.
- Mould into bâtards and prove on a tray for 60 minutes.
- Flour and cut, place in the oven with steam and bake.
- Leave to cool on a wire tray.

Flaviac

La Gare des Douceurs

Shop interior

Sweet chestnuts

Flaviac is a small town in the Ardeche region. It is possible that Bishop Honoré could have travelled through this ancient part of France. Flaviac's claim to fame is that it hasn't one; nothing appears to have happened or nothing that I can find in the history books.

The valley of the Drome has its own agricultural mixture of wheat, lavender, grapes and walnuts. The Ardeche had another; here maize, sweet chestnuts, figs and livestock, mainly cows, provided the local economy. We stopped for coffee on our way up through the winding roads of the Ardeche at Flaviac. It was lunch time and we needed a break so I headed for the local bakery. This is called La Gare des Douceurs; I guess a Station of Memories might fit the translation.

The bakery is a treasure, situated in a building of the French Grande Belle Epoques period. Internally, the shop is decorated with narrow gauge memorabilia. The display counters are narrow gauge railway trucks, mounted on rail track in an L shape in the shop. The trucks have plate glass sheets mounted on top to provide hygienic display cases for the bread, cakes and pastries on sale. On a lower level there is a café facility to consume tart au pomme and coffee. It was in the shop where I had a brief conversation with a local woman. I was greatly impressed by what she had to say. In essence she said that the French produced some of their finest food with ingredients that grew a short distance from their homes.

Bread on sale in the shop amongst the staple baguettes was pain au mais and pain marron et figues all growing locally. After our sandwiches and coffee we left en route for Villefranche.

Close up of the railway truck display

Pain aux Marron et Figues (Sweet Chestnut & Fig)

Ingredients

450g	Wholemeal bread flour
50g	Chestnut flour (roasted)
10g	Yeast fresh
7g	Salt
295g	Water
150g	Pre-fermented dough
30g	Nibbed (roasted) chestnuts
30g	Dried fig (diced small)

Total 1kg 22g

Mixing Method

- Place the flours, water and yeast in a bowl and mix for 5 minutes.
- Cover for 20 minutes.
- Add the pre-fermented dough and the salt which has been dispersed in 5g of warm water taken from the recipe.
- Mix for 8 minutes.
- Rest for 5 minutes.
- Add the nibbed chestnuts and fig to the mixture and mix slowly until the nuts and fruit are well distributed in the dough, or finish it by hand.
- Cool rapidly on a wire tray.

Dough temp:	24°C
Mixing water temp:	_____°C
Mixing time:	5 mins + 8 mins
1st fermentation time:	1 hour
Conditions:	Warm and covered
De-gas/knock back:	45 mins
Scale at:	500g
Yield:	2
Resting period:	10 mins
Tray tin type and size:	38 x 26cm
Warm/prepare:	Lightly greased
Shape and form dough:	Into balls with a small stalk
Prove at:	25°C for 45 mins
Pre-baking finish:	Dust with rye flour and cut with scissors, like a horse chestnut shell, make lots of spikes
Oven temperature:	230°C (fan 220°C)
Baking time:	35 mins
Conditions:	drop to 210°C if over coloured, with humidity for first 25 mins
Post baking finish:	Mist spray exiting the oven

Approximate production time: 3 hours
Product life: 2 days

Sliced and served with brie

Lanuéjouls

The route through the Ardeche is beautiful in the late spring. The roadsides are lined with yellow and blue irises and higher up more varieties of alpine flowers. Over snaking roads and narrow bridges we made this picturesque and yet difficult journey with our big trailer. At the top of a range of high hills the views, I thought, looked like those in the opening scenes of the Sound of Music. Julie Andrews did not burst into song but this could not spoil the beautiful vista for me. From the hills of the Ardeche we travelled through Lozere, another mountainous area, to the Aveyron. Here there are far fewer hills and the landscape changes to meadows. Exhausted by the long drive we pulled off the main road at a village called Lanuéjouls. Camping was advertised on a roadside sign, so we drove into the campsite and quickly set up our trailer.

Jean Luc & Anne Marie Wittner

We awoke the next day and looked out of our camper. In these lush meadows we met our nearest neighbours, seven fawn and white cows all lined up to greet us. Lanuéjouls is mostly on either side of the main road, but it has two bakeries, one is supplied from a manufacturing unit outside of the village in Villefranche, and the other is a family business. The Wittners run their bakery in the traditional way, bakery, shop and home. Artisan bakers, they produce local and regional specialities, the Trefoil and Pave. The pave is bread made with 68% water in the dough and is difficult to handle for the inexperienced bread maker. Pave is cut into long strips and has a long cool fermentation, which produces an internal structure like honeycomb. It can be topped with cheese to become au fromage; eat this with a green salad (dressed with walnut oil) and grilled meat and vegetables from the BBQ.

Shop bought pave

Anne Marie, Jean Luc Wittner and their daughter Céline, have been most helpful. Jean Luc gave me some special cloth lined baskets for proving loaves like the boule, pain couronne. Their week's production was mainly baguettes and flutes from white flour (Monday to Thursday). On Friday the trend changes to speciality breads this gives Jean Luc an opportunity to show his high level craft skills to the full. The weekend will see wonderful loaves two of which you can see in the photograph. Pave and pain campagne and many of the local specialities appear in the shop.

Jean Luc with two grand pains

Pave (Cobble Stone)

Ingredients

500g	Levain
112g	Rye flour
7g	Yeast fresh
460g	Water (24°C)
5g	Black treacle
640g	Wheat bread flour
16g	Salt
5g	Butter (optional)

Total 1.745kg

Dough temp:	20°C
Mixing water temp:	____°C
1st speed mix time:	15 mins (or 20 mins by hand)
1st fermentation time:	3 hours
Conditions:	Cool and dry
De-gas/knock back:	Fold into three after 1 hour and again at 2 hours: Gently pat out at 3 hours
Scale at:	340g approx
Yield:	5 *NB: you will be cutting the dough to size, not weight, so your yield may vary, so 4, 5, or 6 loaves will be O.K*
Tray tin type and size:	38 x 26cm
Warm/prepare:	Grease and flour
Shape and form dough:	Cut into oblongs or squares
Prove at:	25°C for 80 mins
Pre-baking finish:	Dust with light rye flour
Oven temperature:	230°C (fan 220°C)
Baking time:	25 mins
Conditions:	With humidity for 20 mins
Post baking finish:	Dust with flour

Approximate production time: 4 hours 30 mins
Product life: 2 days

Mixing Methods (levain)

- Place the water, treacle and yeast in a bowl.
- Place the salt, rye flour, wheat bread flour, butter and levain in your mixing bowl.
- Disperse the yeast in water.
- Add the liquid to the flours.
- Mix for about 15 minutes (by hand 20 minutes). If too sticky use a little vegetable oil on your hands. Avoid a lot of additional flour as it makes for dry bread.
- Cover and set aside in a warm place for approximately 60 minutes.
- After 1 hour fold the dough over three times to de-gas and equalise the temperature.
- Repeat the above after 2 hours. After 3 hours gently pat out the dough (avoid de-gassing the dough). Cut the dough into oblongs or squares. Place them on prepared trays and prove for about 80 mins at room temperature. Dust them with flour.

Villefranche

Villefranche-de-Rouergue

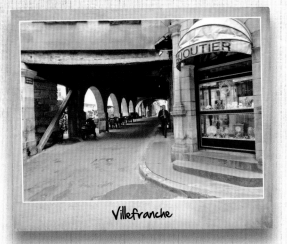

Villefranche

The first town of Villefranche stood on the Roman road from Rodez to Cahors. As an imperial staging post, it would have provided meat and drink for weary travellers. After the Romans left it continued to serve the needs of the new breed of merchants who travelled this road.

Bordering on the Duchy of Aquitaine and the County of Toulouse, Villefranche was in bandit country. In France, Counties and Duchies changed hands through war or marriage settlements or both, the result was that lawlessness was rife. The answer to the regional lawlessness was to build a fortified town. Alphonse, brother to Louis IX (they had a lot of Louis throughout history) did just that in 1252. With stability, the settlement achieved market status and grew into a town.

Villefranche is situated on the confluence of the rivers Aveyron and L' Alzou. The region being named after its principal river the Aveyron, it was this river and road convergence that brought wealth to the town. Having your fortified place by the river and road route gave the nobility control of commerce, travel and taxation.

Bishop Honoré might have passed through the town on his way to the west, and may have preached by the river.

Villefranche is very old and very interesting, because of its 13th century grid pattern layout. Because of this and its narrow roads it is best avoided on market days. Do go and visit this town of covered walkways and tall stone houses. You can appreciate how wild and lawless those days would have been, when you visit the fortified Church of Notre-Dame.

Just out of town, thoughtfully situated at the main road junction, is the new concept in baking sales. The bakery and Salon de Thé is a drive in, place your order, and take tea. When you are ready, pay for your bread, pastries and tea and off you go. A good concept but the bread is not so wonderful, over mixed and under baked; perhaps they were having a bad day. Villefranche historically linked the wheat growing areas on the Quercy causse to the west, with the rye producing areas to the east of Villefranche. My choice of bread is *Pain de Meteil* made from wheat and rye flours

Fortified town

Pain de Méteil (Wheat & Rye Bread)

Ingredients

250g	Strong white bread flour
250g	Light rye flour
310g	Water
10g	Salt
15g	Yeast fresh
150g	Pre-fermented dough

Total 985g

Dough temp:	25°C
Mixing water temp:	_____°C
1st speed mix time:	18 mins (or 20 mins by hand)
1st fermentation time:	70 mins
Conditions:	Ambient and covered
De-gas/knock back:	40 mins
Scale at:	325g
Yield:	3
Resting period:	10 mins
Tray tin type and size:	38 x 26cm
Warm/prepare:	Lightly greased
Shape and form dough:	Into boulot or short bâtard
Prove at:	23°C for 50 - 60 mins
Pre-baking finish:	Dust with rye flour and cut just prior to going into the oven
Oven temperature:	230°C (fan 220°C)
Baking time:	25 - 30 mins
Conditions:	First 20 mins with steam then vent by opening the oven door (with care)
Post baking finish:	None

Approximate production time: 2 hours 30 mins
Product life: 1 - 2 days

Mixing Method

- Place the flours and 300g of water in bowl, mix for 4-5 minutes and then stop.
- Cover the bowl and stand for 15 minutes approximately.
- Disperse the yeast in the remaining water.
- Sprinkle the salt on the 1st stage dough.
- Add the pre-fermented dough and yeast water.
- Mix for 6 minutes and cover.
- Ferment for 70 minutes.
- De-gas after 40 minutes and cover.
- Scale and mould roughly round.
- Cover and rest for 10 minutes.
- Mould round and slightly flatten the ball into a dome shape. Roll out by hand into a boulot or short bâtard
- Dust with rye flour.
- Cover and prove, cut 2/3 times on top just prior to baking

Cahors

Cahors is a town of two halves, the ancient and the modern. For a change I would like to talk about the modern half. Firstly, the town is blessed with some really good bakers and pastry chefs. The one I chose to visit was L' Amandine, a bakery that specialises in crusty breads. L'Amandine is owned and operated by Bruno la Barthe. This man's name summons up images of Knights in armour meeting up to joust for the hand of a fair lady. Fortunately, the mace was in the savoury pastry not in Bruno's hand. The team at L'Amandine make breads with names like L'crousilot, pain du terrior, miche, pave and pain rustique. The shop window had a fine display of breads - a credit to Bruno and his staff.

But wait, I cannot help myself. I must tell you about one of Cahors' favourite sons, Leon Gambetta, a man with a mission. Leon left Cahors at 18 years old to join the legal profession in Paris. He was an ardent patriot and so he became a member of the Legislative Assembly. He took an active part in the downfall of Napoleon III, then in the formation of the New Republic. Later caught up in the siege of Paris he escaped in a hot air balloon, in order that he could organise the formation of the Army of the Loire.

The old town

Cahors is the capital of the Lot Region, its emblem being the fortified bridge across the river (Pont Valentre). Medieval Cahors is a haphazard mix of buildings built of limestone, brick and timber, with roofs of red pan tiles. The almond biscuits called tuilles take their name from these roof tiles. The richer medieval buildings have ornate carved wooden supports and beam ends, so keep an eye out for these and don't do as I did and fall over as I gazed at the carvings. Cahors has had its bad times one of these being caused by the scourge of vines, Phylloxera. Happily, modern controls and roses have kept the vines clean. Money has returned to Cahors and many of the medieval buildings are being renovated, correctly and sympathetically, to bring them back from the brink of terminal decay.

Pain aux cereales proving

Pain aux Ceriales

Ingredients

250g	Strong white bread flour
125g	Whole grain rye flour
100g	Whole grain spelt flour
50g	Oat flour*
20g	Malted barley flour*
10g	Salt
150g	Levain
10g	Yeast fresh
290g	Water
10g	Golden linseed
10g	Sunflower seeds
5g	Sesame seeds (for decoration)

Total 1.3kg

Dough temp:	25°C
Mixing water temp:	_____°C
1st speed mix time:	16 mins + 2 mins (or 20 mins by hand)
1st fermentation time:	90 mins
Conditions:	Warm and covered
De-gas/knock back:	60 mins
Scale at:	500g
Yield:	2
Resting period:	10 mins
Tray tin type and size:	Oven tile or 38 x 26cm tray
Shape and form dough:	Into bâtards
Prove at:	25°C for up to 75 mins, or until double the original size
Pre-baking finish:	Mist spray with water and decorate with sesame seeds, cut lengthways
Oven temperature:	230°C (fan 220°C)
Baking time:	40 mins
Conditions:	Humidity, water bath in base of the oven

Approximate production time: 4 hours 25 mins
Product life: 2 days

Mixing Method

- Place all the ingredients in a mixing bowl with the salt and levain, except the seeds.
- Dissolve the yeast in the water at 38°C.
- Add to the dry ingredients.
- Mix for 16 minutes on slow, or by hand for 20 minutes.
- Rest for 5 minutes.
- Add the linseeds and sunflower seeds.
- Mix for 2 minutes slow.
- Ferment in a bowl for 90 minutes, covered.
- De-gas after 60 minutes.
- Scale at 500g.
- Mould round, rest for 10 minutes.
- Shape into bâtards
- Prove on a tray or in a basket.

* If you find it difficult to find oat flour and malted wheat flour, use an electric coffee grinder to reduce rolled oats and malted grains to coarse flour for inclusion in the recipe.

Argentat

Argentat developed on the banks of the river Dordogne. Because of its trade with England it grew rich. The town's earliest beginning in industry and trade was in metal work and it famously prospered with its forges. The ore for this trade came from across the sea in England and more specifically Cornwall. The town has a museum which houses an exhibition of artefacts recovered by the local archaeologists. On the floor they display a quern and a small mill stone, both hand operated, back breaking work for someone grinding grain to make bread.

Argentat like so many other places was caught up in religious wars. The town was for many years a Protestant religious centre, with Royal patronage to support the town both in trade and with their religious conviction. Wars broke out between Catholics and Protestants; the Catholics won the majority of the battles and established themselves as the victors.

We camped on the banks of the river Dordogne for two nights. The next day we set out to explore this charming part of France. Argentat was our nearest town and happily it was market day. The market was different from many of the others we had visited. Blocks of Pain d'Epice, not strictly bread, was on sale. Other stalls had honey and the spices to make it.

Cottage near Argentat

Pain d' Epice is made in other areas and there are many recipes, this is the one that best represents the Dordogne for me.

If you take the road up the hill out of Argentat you will come to the bakery of Jean-Luc. We visited him on Sunday morning and he was finishing off his customers orders. Jean-Luc has an interesting system; each customer must have a couple of traditional bread sacks with their names on. They place their orders with him and pick up the sack with the bread in when they call the next day, leaving the empty one for the next order.

Jean-Luc and the Grand Couronne

Le pain pick up point

Pain d' Epice

Ingredients

225g	Milk
450g	Clear honey
120g	Butter
30g	Yeast fresh
300g	Whole eggs (x6 - average weight 50g)
45g	Dark brown sugar
300g	White cake flour
150g	Brown bread flour
15g	Salt
10g	Baking powder
10g	Bicarbonate of soda
100g	Spice blend
20g	Orange & lemon (finely cut)

Total 1.775kg

Batter temp:	21°C
1st speed mix time:	3 + 2 + 6 + 6 mins (17 mins)
Scale at:	590g
Yield:	3
Tray tin type and size:	22cm x 11cm long with 2 paper liner, bread/cake tin
Prove at:	25°C for 20 mins
Pre-baking finish:	None
Oven temperature:	150°C (fan 140°C)
Baking time:	45 - 55 mins
Conditions:	Moist heat
Cooling:	On wire tray

Approximate production time: 1 hour
Product life: 12 days

Mixing Method

Stage 1

- Place the milk, honey and butter in a saucepan, warm only, and maximum 50°C.

NB. make sure the mixture is cooled a little before adding the yeast.

Stage 2

- Place the eggs and sugar in a separate bowl and whisk together for 3 minutes

Stage 3

- Sieve all the dry ingredients together and place on a sheet of greaseproof paper.
- Put stage 1 in a mixing bowl with beater attachment; mix on slow speed or by hand for 2 minutes.
- Feed the dry ingredients on the paper into the machine, (or by hand) for 6 minutes. Avoid forming lumps.
- Add the eggs and sugar in 3 - 4 lots, scraping the sides of the bowl in between additions with a spatula, mix thoroughly between each addition for 6 minutes.

Production Notes

- Stop the machine and scrape the sides of the bowl at regular intervals before adding the spices. You can increase the amounts or change the spices to suit your taste. Put all the spices into a bowl and mix. Before adding the blend to the cake mixture, mix in thoroughly 2 tablespoons of the cake mixture to the spices, this will stop any lumps forming and aid distribution throughout the mixture.
- Place the mixture in a paper lined long boat tin and stand for 20 minutes prior to baking.
- Before baking loafs put a baking tin with boiling water in it on the floor of the oven. Because honey will burn above 160°C avoid turning the heat up. If high colour is observed cover loafs with a sheet of grease proof paper (if non fan) or turn the oven down. Loafs tend to flower (split open on top).

The Spices

20g	Zest of 1 lemon and 1 orange
6g	Ground cinnamon (2 heaped teaspoons)
2g	Ground cumin (1 level teaspoon)
3g	½ nutmeg ground (or 1 heaped teaspoon)
100g	Fresh root ginger (chopped and reduced to a paste*)

A coffee grinder will reduce root ginger to paste

Limoges

Like so many towns and cities in France, Limoges traces its origins to it being a fording place by the river Vienne. The Romans used it as part of their highway system, running from the east to the west. Even better the town sat astride the important North-South trade routes from the Mediterranean. The inhabitants had the best of all worlds sitting on the major trading routes of the period, they became prosperous. Add a small venerated relic and you had a winning hand. The Abbey of Saint Martial was sited on the grave of Martial; a 3rd century missionary. Limoges had arrived. By the 11th century Limoges was a well establish part of the pilgrim's route to Spain.

Limoges shouts porcelain vases and antiques. In the early 19th century the commercial centre of porcelain was established. Here thousands of horse drawn wagons transported these products along the road network. Unlike our potters who turned to the canals for transport the French endured the breakages that must have occurred.

August Renoir was born here in 1841 he is perhaps the most famous of the impressionists. Limoges has plenty of wonderful buildings to see and a good selection of Boulanger's to visit both in the city and château districts.

The water gate

Proving pain de seigle

A fine example of commercial light rye bread

Pain de Seigle (Rye Bread)

Ingredients

165g	Strong white bread flour
325g	Wholemeal rye flour
345g	Water
165g	Pre-fermented dough
10g	Salt
10g	White wine vinegar
15g	Yeast fresh
5g	Sugar
10g	Butter
0.5g	Ground caraway seeds* (for decoration)

Total 1.5kg

Caraway seeds can be used sparingly with rye

Dough temp:	23°C
Mixing water temp:	_____°C
1st speed mix time:	5 mins
2nd speed mix time:	6 mins (or 20 mins by hand)
1st fermentation time:	50 mins
Conditions:	Warm and covered
De-gas/knock back:	25 mins
Scale at:	500g
Yield:	2
Resting period:	10 mins
Tray tin type and size:	38 x 26cm
Warm/prepare:	Lightly greased
Shape and form dough:	Round or bâtard
Prove at:	25°C for 1 hour
Pre-baking finish:	Dust with rye flour, shallow cut diagonally and bake immediately with humidity
Oven temperature:	230°C (fan 220°C)
Baking time:	45 mins
Conditions:	Steam for 35 mins, 10 mins dry bake
Post baking finish:	Mist spray immediately exit the oven

Approximate production time: 3 hours 30 mins
Product life: 2 - 3 days

Mixing Method

- Place the flours, pre-fermented dough, salt and butter in a mixing bowl.
- Place in a jug the yeast, sugar and white wine vinegar with the water (38°C).
- Stir for 30 seconds to disperse the yeast.
- Add to the mixing bowl with the dry ingredients.
- Mix for 5 minutes slowly.
- Mix for 6 minutes on medium speed.
- Cover the bowl and ferment for 50 minutes.
- De-gas after 20 minutes.
- Scale and mould round.
- Rest for 10 minutes.
- Mould into final shape.
- Place in a proving basket in a warm area of the kitchen and cover.

Poitiers

Founded in the Gallo-Roman period, it has one of the most venerated Christian buildings in France, the "Baptistery of Saint Jean". The Baptistery was built in the 4th century, restored in the 10th century and must have been visited by Bishop Honoré. Evangelising and baptising was his mission, so I feel sure he would have wetted or immersed a few converts there.

Poitiers was for many years an English possession ceded to the Crown as part of Eleanor of Aquitaine's estates and properties. It passed to the French crown, only to be lost again to the English by Jean II (the good) defeated on a misty autumn day. It was the 19th September 1356 when the Black Prince's forces took the field and by late afternoon, as the light fell, it was all over. The outcome of the battles was decided by the English archers and the long bow, the French archers having crossbows.

The French could load and fire at best three bolts per minute, the English could launch up to seven. A hail of arrows and the French would have been on the wrong end of a thousand sharp points. It is interesting to note the number of names associated with this fearsome weapon. Archer, Bowman Rodgers, Gauche - Rodger (left handed archer, la Gauche), Arrowsmith and Fletcher to name but a few. Archery, practiced every Sunday on the village green, paid dividends that day. Naturally the French took it back in 1372 and this sort of thing apparently was repeated up and down France.

A Royal on horse back

A view from the Château

1000 years of travel

It was at Poitiers that the favourite of the French forces and their pin-up, Joan of Arc, was subjected to an extremely tough ecclesiastical examination. Joan came through it with flying colours. The Bishops felt a little threatened by this young woman, in fact they were not the only ones to feel threatened and later, when she was wounded at Saint Honoré's gate, she was handed over to the British by elements acting for the French crown, convicted and burnt at the stake.

Pain Complete (Wholemeal)

Ingredients

500g	Wholemeal bread flour
300g	Water (38°C)
125g	Pre-fermented dough
10g	Salt*
5g	Yeast fresh
15g	Treacle (optional)
10g	Butter (optional)

Total 965g

Mixing Method

- Place flour, water, pre-fermented dough and yeast into a bowl and mix slowly for 10 minutes, or by hand for 10 minutes.
- Add the salt (*which is softened in 5g of hot water) to the dough.
- Mix for another 10 minutes, or by hand for 15 minutes.
- Treacle and butter can be added to extent the shelf life of the bread.
- Ferment covered for 60 - 80 minutes, de-gas and scale.
- Shape into bâtards or boules.
- Flour and prove.
- Cut the dough very lightly with a sharpened blade.

Dough temp:	23°C
Mixing water temp:	_____°C
1st speed mix time:	10 mins
2nd speed mix time:	10 mins (or 25 mins by hand)
1st fermentation time:	60 - 80 mins
Conditions:	Ambient and covered
De-gas/knock back:	30 mins
Scale at:	450g
Yield:	2
Resting period:	10 mins
Tray tin type and size:	Baking tray or loaf tin (480g)
Warm/prepare:	Lightly greased
Shape and form dough:	Into bâtards or boules
Prove at:	21°C for 60 - 90 mins
Pre-baking finish:	Flour, lightly cut diagonal lines into the top of the dough
Oven temperature:	230°C (fan 210°C)
Baking time:	40 mins
Conditions:	Moist heat using water bath in the bottom of the oven

Approximate production time: 2 hours 40 mins
Product life: 2 days (3 - 4 days with treacle & butter)

Saumur

Saumur the town is built high up on the hillside, to be kept safe from the winter floods. In the early years of the town's development, it was a fording place across the Loire followed by the needy construction of a bridge which enhanced the town's reputation. Finally being on the route Saint Jacque de Compostela and Saumur's fame was complete.

The Château Fort of Saumur built in the 14th century sits majestically on the chalky outcrop that overlooks the river. There are fine views from the château, flanked on one side by the old town and vineyards on the other. There are many Boulanger's working in the old town, these produce traditional overnight doughs and quality pastries. Saumur is famous for horses, wine, the military and its renowned tank museum (the best I have ever visited).

The Pilgrims route, over land and via the river, the château and green figs. These are the photographic memories of the Loire.

Château Saumur

Another view of Château Saumur

Early morning dew

Pain de Gruau

Ingredients

500g	Best white bread flour
325g	Water
7g	Yeast fresh
7g	Salt
10g	Milk powder
3g	Malt extract or black treacle
25g	Butter
175g	Pre-fermented dough

Total 1.52kg

Mixing Method (straight dough)

- Add all the ingredients to the bowl, including the treacle, with the water and mix for 4 minutes, clear the bowl sides.
- Mix for a further 4 minutes on 2nd or medium speed, or by hand 8 for minutes.
- Add the pre-fermented dough and mix for 5 minutes on slow.
- Cover and ferment for 95 minutes.
- De-gas after 45 minutes
- Scale into rounds and rest for 5 - 10 minutes
- Mould into short bâtards or small units of 70g.
- Place on warm prepared trays or on a linen cloth. Prove for 60 minutes.
- Bake and cool.

Dough temp:	24°C
Mixing water temp:	_____°C
1st speed mix time:	4 mins + 5 mins
2nd speed mix time:	4 mins (or 8 mins by hand)
1st fermentation time:	95 mins
Conditions:	Cover, warm place
De-gas/knock back:	45 mins
Scale at:	70g - 15 rolls or 175g for 6 short bâtards
Resting period:	5 - 10 mins
Tray tin type and size:	38 x 26cm
Warm/prepare:	Lightly greased
Shape and form dough:	Into baguettes or rolls
Prove at:	27°C for 1 hour
Pre-baking finish:	Rolls: 1 cut Bâtards: 3 - 4 cuts
Oven temperature:	230°C (fan 220°C)
Baking time:	Rolls: 8 - 10 mins Bâtards: 18 - 20 mins
Conditions:	Rolls: Steam for 5 mins Bâtards: Steam for 8 mins
Post baking finish:	Butter glaze

Approximate production time: 4 hours
Product life: 2 days

Short bâtard

Angers

Angers is a most imposing place, a city even in Bishop Honoré's time. It is a city of rivers and history. Rivers, because the Sarthe, Mayenne and Oudon join with the mighty Loire here and history, well the Romans built a fort at Angers; the present Château-Fort sits on the Roman foundations. This place oozes history out of its ancient stones. For instance, in June 1129 Geoffrey Plantagenet married William the Conqueror's granddaughter, the proud Matilde, their inheritance being England and Normandy. Henry II and Eleanor of Aquitaine also tied the knot here.

Shop interior

Richard Raune and staff

On our visit with the Marquis Charles-Andre de Brissac, he was kind enough to make an appointment with Richard Raune the baker. Richard's bakery is a high quality establishment close to the Loire. Jenny and I arrived with me clutching my copy of *Les Pains Français*. As we walked in the shop and introduced ourselves, Richard remarked "I'm in that book".
It appeared that most of the photographs of hands producing the many types of bread are his. My friend Gregory was tutored in baking by one of the two authors of this book. The expression 'it's a small world' comes to mind.

In fact it was Gregory who arranged for my students and I to visit the Paris bakery school and it sparked my interest in St. Honoré and French breads.

The Château-Fort lies alongside the ancient city, its massive walls and fortified turrets dominating the whole area. In WW2 the Polish Government set up their head quarters in Angers. They didn't stay long and had to retreat to London. Angers has some interesting bakeries, patisseries and chocolatiers in the old city. They are well worth a visit and parking seems to be accessible most days.

Ovens

Pain au Mais (Cornbread)

Ingredients

450g	Extra strong bread flour
112g	Mais flour
150g	Milk
75g	Water
90g	Eggs (x2, small)
45g	Granulated sugar
7g	Salt
15g	Yeast fresh
60g	Unsalted butter*
120g	Drained tinned sweet corn

Total 1.124kg

If salted butter is used reduce the salt by 2g.

Dough temp:	24°C
Mixing water temp:	_____°C
1st speed mix time:	20 mins (or 20 mins by hand)
1st fermentation time:	40 mins
Conditions:	Warm and covered
De-gas/knock back:	20 mins
Scale at:	280g x3 cobs, 90g x1 leaves
Yield:	3
Resting period:	10 mins
Tray tin type and size:	38 x 26cm
Warm/prepare:	Lightly greased
Shape and form dough:	280g x3 into balls, 90g x1
Prove at:	25°C for 1 hour
Pre-baking finish:	Roll 90g balls into a strip and 280g balls into a corn shape (see diagram)
Oven temperature:	220°C (fan 210°C)
Baking time:	25 mins
Conditions:	With humidity
Post baking finish:	Exit the oven brush melted butter glaze on the cob only

Approximate production time: 3 hours
Product life: 2 - 3 days

Mixing Method

- Mix the flours, milk and water together for 3 minutes slow speed or by hand.
- Add the eggs, sugar, and salt and mix for 2 minutes slow speed or by hand.
- Finally add the yeast and softened butter on slow speed and mix for 15 minutes or by hand.
- Cover and rest for 5 minutes.
- Add the sweet corn by hand to avoid damage to the corn.
- Cover and ferment for 40 minutes.
- De-gas after 20 minutes.
- After 40 minutes scale and mould roughly.
- Rest for 10 minutes.
- Re-shape into corn cob shapes.
- 90g of dough is rolled out on a floured surface to give 9/10 triangles for the stylised corn leaves.
- Moisten the cobs and attach the leaves. The points should be curled over a little.
- Brush with rice paste.**
- Cover and prove for 60 minutes.
- Bake.

**Rice paste		
55g	Water (38°C)	Mix ingredients together and stand for 30 minutes fermentation before applying to the corn cob with a suitable brush.
2g	Yeast	
2g	Sugar	
4g	Corn oil	
55g	Rice Flour	

Le Mont Saint-Michel

Statue of Joan of Arc

Le Mont Saint-Michel was a major Christian site in Bishop Honoré's day. In fact being one of France's most influential Christian places of pilgrimage, then and now. The abbey started as an oratory in the 8th century, Aubert Bishop of Avaranches claimed that Saint Michel appeared in a vision, one night as he was praying. Aubert said that in his visitation he was instructed to build a church on the mount. Building work started on the island with a modest abbey church and it was from this building that the abbey you see today has evolved.

As you approach the abbey across the wind swept low lands of the coast, it is possible to imagine the affect this building would have had on a 9th century pilgrim. Le Mont Saint-Michel is a hill sticking out of the sandy flat lands and looks like it has been transported from the Alps. In the 9th century pilgrims visited this holy place and would have been given hospitality by the resident monks. This was (and still is) a bleak place, the wind from *la Manche* (sea) must have chilled the occupants to the bone.

Sadly today there is no bread baked on the island by the 6 monks and 6 nuns who reside there.

Le Mont Saint-Michel has been built and rebuilt, and further fortified to keep out the enemy (the British). Blockaded and attacked, it never fell. Joan of Arc was aware of its potency and used its name in her rallying cry for battle. The wounded Joan was captured at St. Honoré's gate in Paris, she was handed over by the French to the British, to be tried, who then burnt her at the stake. This was like being handed a poisoned chalice for the British. There is a fine golden statue of Joan on a horse in Paris and another of her standing wearing armour about half way up the hill at Le Mont Saint-Michel.

I am sure that in the 11th century there would have been relics to see and touch. Indulgences and lead seals to be obtained, bottles of water blessed by the Bishop. Now the lower third of the Island has many eating houses and souvenir shops. Pilgrims now arrive from all over the world. Coach loads in fact arrive on the shuttle bus service, delivered to the entrance. I wonder what Bishop Aubert and Honoré would have thought about their island in the 21st century.

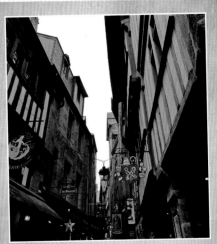

Ancient street

The chapel

Pain au Herbes

Ingredients

350g	White bread flour
150g	Light rye flour
5g	Dried rubbed thyme
7g	Dried rubbed fennel
10g	Sesame
10g	Salt
8g	Yeast fresh
310g	Water
200g	Pre-fermented dough

Total 1.5kg

Dough temp:	25°C
Mixing water temp:	_____ °C
1st speed mix time:	10 mins + 10 mins (or 20 mins by hand)
1st fermentation time:	90 mins
Conditions:	Cool, ambient
De-gas/knock back:	45 mins
Scale at:	340g
Yield:	3
Resting period:	10 mins
Tray tin type and size:	38 x 26cm
Warm/prepare:	With oil
Shape and form dough:	Into balls, then oval shapes
Prove at:	25°C for 1 hour
Pre-baking finish:	**A**. Spray with water and roll in sesame seeds at shape and form, or **B**. Spray and sprinkle with sesame seeds just prior to baking
Oven temperature:	230°C (fan 220°C)
Baking time:	20 - 25 mins
Conditions:	Steam for 15 mins
Post baking finish:	Exit oven mist spray with water

Approximate production time: 3 hours 30 mins
Product life: 2 days

Mixing Method

- Place all the dry ingredients, including the herbs, in the bowl.
- Disperse the yeast in the water.
- Mix for 10 minutes on slow or by hand.
- Add the pre-fermented dough in 50g portions.
- Mix for a further 10 minutes on slow speed, or by hand.
- Cover and ferment for 90 minutes.
- De-gas after 45 minutes.
- Scale at 340g.
- Mould round.
- Rest for 10 minutes.
- Roll into an oval shape.
- Prove for 60 minutes
- Spray lightly with water.
- Sprinkle sesame on the surface of the dough.
- Cut the surface with the sign of the cross.
- Put immediately in the oven

Brissac-Quincé

Château Brissac

Storms on the Atlantic coast at Carnac drove us inland to Brissac. Wind swept refugees, we arrived in the Brissac area looking for a camp site. Improving weather gave us an opportunity to set up camp and explore. We arrived on market day, the streets and the place had all the classic ingredients and materials, all the stalls I love; fish, cheese, meats, bread and lots of fresh vegetables for sale. The town of Brissac is like so many ancient towns, built on the high ground to avoid flooding.

Our first meal in the town was at a small restaurant halfway up the hill, ham and cheese galettes, wonderful. The view from the restaurant window is of the château at Brissac, standing at the bottom of the hill. The château is renowned for being one of the tallest châteaux in the Loire region. The château and the town appear to be approximately equal in height neither being over looked. The château is owned and lived in by the family of the Marquise de Brissac. Charles-Andre de Brissac the owner is a very busy man. At the time of our last visit he

was directing the work force working on a large part of the exterior of the château. The château is my favourite as it is loved and lived in as well as being accessible.

I could not find a bread recipe that I felt represented the château and the town, so I have created one. It contains local grown ingredients, including dried grapes, hazelnuts and quincé. I posted Charles-Andre a loaf named Château de Brissac from Yorkshire. I do not think it arrived in prime condition, but he was none the less complimentary about it. On one of our visits we were able to make an appointment with him. We talked about my book and the reason for writing it. It was then that he told me that his family had held the Royal Warrant *"Les Pourvoyeurs de pain du Roi"* Boulanger to the King. I could tell you about the hot air balloon rallies and the history of this château.
For more details, visit the website:
www.chateau-brissac.fr.

Charles-Andre de Brissac

Ovens of the château

Charles-Andre, the château and the ovens, as sent by C-A.

Pain Château Brissac

Ingredients

Poolish

250g	Extra strong white flour
200g	Milk (38°C)
3g	Yeast fresh

Dough

300g	Extra strong flour
5g	Salt
75g	Sugar
100g	Butter (24°C)
35g	Egg yolks
12g	Yeast fresh
65g	Water (38°C)
200g	Best quality sultanas*
30g	Ground almonds
50g	Quince*
50g	Roast nibbed hazel nuts

Total 1.375kg

Poolish temp:	38°C
Dough temp:	25°C
1st speed mix time:	20 mins (or 20 mins by hand)
1st fermentation time:	2 hours
Conditions:	Warm and covered
De-gas/knock back:	1 hour
Scale at:	680g
Yield:	2
Resting period:	15 mins
Tray tin type and size:	38 x 26cm or a long tin
Warm/prepare:	Lightly greased
Shape and form dough:	Into bâtards, or place into a long bread tin
Prove at:	25°C for 75 - 80 mins
Pre-baking finish:	None
Oven temperature:	185°C (fan 175°C)
Baking time:	30 - 35 mins
Conditions:	With humidity
Post baking finish:	Glaze with honey & orange juice (2tsp orange 1tsp honey) from the oven

Approximate production time: 3 hours 30 mins
Product life: 7 days

Mixing Method

- Mix together the flour milk and yeast in a bowl, cover and set aside in a warm place for 3 hours.
- Place the flour, salt, butter and yeast in a mixing bowl.
- Rub through the butter with your fingers, for 3 minutes.
- Put the tepid water, sugar and egg yolk together in a jug and mix to dissolve the sugar.
- Add the egg and water phase to the poolish, then add the liquid to the flour and butter.
- Mix for 20 minutes on slow or by hand.
- Ferment for 2 hours.
- De-gas after 1 hour.
- Scale and shape roughly and rest for 15 mins.
- Re- shape into a bâtard the length of your tin, gently remove any fruit that sticks out of the top of the dough as this will burn during baking.
- Prove for 75 - 80 mins.

Quince cooked lightly in sugar. Sultanas soaked in the juice of the cooked quince for 12 hours or overnight.

Château Pimpean

Château Pimpean stands on the crest of a hill, this raised ground is shale, and it is this stony soil that gives the wine produced at the château its unique flavour. Unlike the other vineyards that grow their vines on chalk. The château produces a fine Anjou wine, Cuvee Passion, I am not a wine expert but I feel that this is a unique wine and should be a on the sampling list for wine connoisseurs. The angel on the bottle's label can also be found on the ceiling of the château's chapel. Cuvee Passion is a very special wine and my only regret is I did not bring more bottles back to England. The wine is grown and bottled at the château. After the harvest is finished Maryset and her family and friends have a harvest supper. The ancient Roman style oven is lit with wood and allowed to burn for some hours before the meal is served. As the embers die down fouees (small breads) are placed at the entrance to the oven. Fouees have their origins in fast food for hungry children; they are fermented dough balls, the remnants of the main batch of bread. These were baked off quickly to satisfy starving children. My experience of children when I am baking is that they are always starving, so nothing changes!

The château is an imposing building that has been neglected in the past; this is no longer the case. Maryset Tugendhat and her husband not only run the vineyard and produce an exceptional wine, they are conservationists too. Maryset was kind enough to take Jenny and I around the château; the buildings are a work in progress. With the tithe barn restored it is now available as a wedding venue. Other rooms have been sympathetically renovated and are a delight to see. Other areas of the château are waiting for the funds to proceed with the restoration work. To restore a building of this age and quality requires lots of money also the passion and drive to see it through. The Tugendhats are those people and I know the château is in safe hands.

The drive up to Château Pimpean

As a baker I made a special request to see the ovens of the château, they are in remarkable good order for their age. The construction is like that of an igloo inside. If you are in the Loire and seeking places of interest that are not on the well worn tourist route, do pay this one a visit. There is a web page that has a presentation that I would not attempt to better; it gives you all you need to know to make an informed choice of interesting days wine hunting.

I was on my way to Château Pimpean when I came across wild garlic, herbs and the curious Cholet cow, that is how the idea for Pain Pimpean was conceived. This light savoury brioche is to be found on the opposite page and it's dedicated to the château that bares its name.

Chapel roof

View of the court yard and château

Maryset Tugendhat

Pain Château Pimpean (Savory Brioche)

Ingredients

500g	Extra strong white flour
50g	Milk (38°C)
20g	Yeast fresh
10g	Salt
2g	Madras curry powder
2g	Course ground black pepper
280g	Eggs (38°C)
140g	Butter (room temperature)

Total 1.04kg

Dough temp:	24°C
Mixing water temp:	_____°C
1st speed mix time:	15 mins (or by hand)
2nd speed mix time:	5 - 7 mins (or 10 mins by hand)
1st fermentation time:	90 mins
Conditions:	Ambient and covered
De-gas/knock back:	45 mins
Scale at:	250g
Yield:	4
Resting period:	10 mins
Tray tin type and size:	38 x 26cm
Warm/prepare:	Lightly greased
Shape and form dough:	Into an oval, as described
Prove at:	25°C for 45 mins
Pre-baking finish:	See mixing method
Oven temperature:	220°C (fan 210°C)
Baking time:	25 mins
Conditions:	With humidity
Post baking finish:	Brush the baked surface with melted butter

Approximate production time: 3 hours
Product life: 2 days

Mixing Method

- Put flour, yeast, salt, Madras curry powder and black pepper in a bowl.
- Warm the egg and milk to 38°C then place with the dry ingredients.
- Mix on slow speed or by hand 15 minutes to form a well developed dough.
- When the dough is ready add the butter in small lumps, mix it in then beat on medium speed for 5 - 7 minutes, 10 minutes by hand to produce a smooth silky dough.
- Cover and ferment for 90 minutes.
- De-gas after 45 minutes. Scale after 90 minutes.
- Mould round and rest.
- Roll into a long oval shape, cut 5cm slit at each end and tease out the dough and curl (see photo).
- Using a fork, make perforations inside edge of dough. This will create a raised lip to contain the filling.
- Lay wild garlic leaves, also called "Ramsons", on the dough, and then spread the leaves with cottage cheese or Quark.
- Spinach leaves can be used if wild garlic leaves are not available; just smear the base with garlic purée. Decorate with cherry tomatoes etc, serve with fresh basil leaves.
- This brioche can be served hot or cold as a snack with a green salad and walnut oil dressing.

Baked with ham & cheese

Argentan

Argentan is a historic town, with many links through its Kings and Queens of England. Guillame le Conquerant had a residence at Falaise. He did not stay around long because he was away over in England bashing the poor Saxons. He left the administration of Normandy to his wife, Queen Maude. She may also have visited the town of Argentan.

In 1944 the town was at the head of the Falaise box, here the retreating German army became trapped between the allied armies. The United States and British troops held the flanks and base that encircled the German army. At the head of the box stood the Poles and the Canadians. The German 2nd Panzer division of mechanized troops, tanks and armoured vehicles attacked the Poles at Mont Ormel. The Poles suffered the loss of many men and tanks but would not give way. Many of the German Generals, officers and staff slipped through and away at night. For the Germans it was a major blow, they lost hundreds of tanks and guns, the official estimates stating that 75,000 men were lost, wounded or captured. The German army was on the run in France but as the allied armies chased the Germans their supply line became longer and longer. Finally the allied armies had to call a halt as they began to run out of fuel and supplies. This gave the Germans the time to re-group, but that's another story.

Fresh bread from the oven

Argentan has an interesting bakery towards the south of the town, modern in layout but different because of the design of the oven. This oven has a rotating base built into a round brick oven housing. The front half of the oven and its door are located in the shop for all to see! Customers can view bread being set on the oven sole and in time removed for sale. This is a definite crowd pleaser, with fascinated customers waiting for the bread to be baked and removed from the oven. Argentan has an open-air market, with a bread stall, and this has a superb display of local bread. Everything in Normandy has apples worked into it if possible, the culinary term, Normand, meaning made with or from apples. Cider came from here, pork and apples, enough said!

Shop with the circular oven

Cider apples

La Tabatière aux Pommes

Ingredients

Stage 1

400g	Bread flour
225g	Water (25°C)
5g	Salt
75g	Pre-fermented dough

Sub total 705g

Stage 2

500g	Bread flour
250g	Rye flour
30g	Black treacle
450g	Water and cider (50:50)
10g	Salt
15g	Yeast fresh

Total 1.96kg

Dough temp:	22°C
Mixing water temp:	_____°C
1st speed mix time:	7 mins + 10 mins
1st fermentation time:	90 mins
Conditions:	Warm and covered
De-gas/knock back:	45 mins
Scale at:	390g
Yield:	5
Resting period:	10 mins
Tray tin type and size:	38 x 26cm
Warm/prepare:	Lightly greased
Shape and form dough:	Into balls - into tabatières
Prove at:	25°C for 75 mins
Pre-baking finish:	See diagram
Oven temperature:	230°C (fan 220°C)
Baking time:	20 - 25 mins
Conditions:	With steam for 15 mins
Post baking finish:	Light spray with water exiting the oven

Approximate production time: 3 hours 30 mins
Product life: 2 days

Mixing Method

- Mix the first stage and place in a container with space to expand and cover for 18 hours at 15°C.

- Mix the ingredients of stage 2 for 7 minutes to form dough.
- Add stage 1 to stage 2 and mix for 8 - 10 mins.
- Cover and ferment for 90 minutes.
- Scale at 390g , mould round and rest for 10 minutes.

Notes

See bread shapes page for details.

Sliced apple can be placed under the flap of the dough and a slice on the top for decoration.

Creating the flap of the tabatière

Assembling the tabatière

Bayeux

Bayeux is the old capital of the Bessin district. Bayeux (pronounced *Bayoo*) is wrapped up with English history: the account for the Norman invasion of England is held here, the relics that Harold swore his oath on are still there and the *Tapisserie de la Reine Mathilde*, or in English the famous Bayeux Tapestry, is well worth a visit. The story it tells was commissioned by William's half brother Odo, then Bishop of Rouen. The embroidery is a masterpiece, of that there is no doubt, even the naughty bits. As in all of human history, the victors have written their account of what happened on the day. In any case, William was victorious and anyone who thinks the women who sewed the tapestry would have dared to say otherwise should look to the Norman treatment of the north of England, or the harrowing of the north, to see what happened when people disagreed with William. Other local attractions include the cathedral Notre-Dame in Bayeux, with its delightful angel musicians in the crypt.

Bayeux was to be witness to another later invasion. In 1944 on June 7th, it was the first French town to be liberated by the Allies, in this case the Canadians. Bayeux was miraculously unscathed as Hitler had still believed that the main invasion force would come in the Pas-de-Calais region. As a result, his crack tank units had been concentrated in the wrong place - oops! Would Hitler have put that in his memoirs if he had won the war? I think not, somehow.

In Bayeux, I visited Eric Litzellmann, a new entrant to the bread making industry. Not fettered by old style beliefs, he set about making traditional bread with a 21st century game plan. After completing his French national service, Eric and his wife started their business with the help of a loan from a local flour miller, who showed sound commercial sense in funding the baker to start and ensuring himself a customer. Eric has since paid off his loan and now of course makes lots of dough (pun intended). His core business is based on "traditional", a legal term for bread made without chemicals and additives. He also still has a lucrative *Agriculture Biologique* market that he makes separately from his traditional breads. The AB products are the same as our organic Soil Association Assured status. That status not only include the flour but also covers the eggs, fruit, nuts, which must all comply with the demands of the AB system.

Eric's bakery is at the Place du Bois but his sales team extend their range by attending the Marche pleinair (out door markets) all around the Normandy coast and up the Carentan Peninsula to St. Mere Eglise. Interestingly, in the D-Day landings a paratrooper from the 101st Airborne got snagged on the roof while making his perilous descent: I hope they've got him down now as he must be getting a bit cold*. Anyway, Eric's special brioche, of his own invention, is a standard brioche with an equal dough weight of butter laminated into it. Use Danish butter, not English, Irish or New Zealand as they are all too soft and above all do not use one of those spreads that thinks it's butter.

The old town of Bayeux

Bayeux Cathedral

Relics of La Bienheureuse Catherine de St-Augustin

*They have: I'm reliably informed that he's now been replaced by a commemorative dummy, thank goodness.

Brioche Litzellmann

Ingredients

250g	Strong white bread flour
20g	Milk
1g	Yeast fresh
8g	Salt
25g	Sugar
135g	Eggs
200g	Levain natural
20g	Danish butter (cold)
30g	Zest and juice of half a lemon

Sub total 689g

360g	Danish butter (chilled)

Total 1.49kg

Dough temp:	25°C
Mixing water temp:	_____°C
1st speed mix time:	3 mins + 12 mins
1st fermentation time:	20 mins + 20 mins (Refrigerate for 24 hours)
Conditions:	24°C if possible
Scale at:	335g
Yield:	3
Resting period:	30 mins + 15 mins + 15 mins
Tray tin type and size:	20 x 10cm baking tins
Shape and form dough:	Pat the dough out to enable you to cut 3 pieces to suit the tins sizes.
Prove at:	26°C for 4 hours
Pre-baking finish:	Egg and milk wash, put in oven immediately
Oven temperature:	220°C for 10 mins, then 180°C for 15 mins
Baking time:	25 mins
Conditions:	Need a hot oven to start the lift, and then reduce to 180°C to finish. Cover if necessary.
Post baking finish:	Tip the tin to remove any excess butter/oil on exiting the oven before removing the brioche.

Approximate production time: 10 hours
Product life: 5 days

Mixing method

- Place all the ingredients in a bowl and mix slowly for 3 minutes or by hand.
- Rest for 15 minutes. Adjust the consistency if necessary.
- Mix for 12 minutes on slow speed or by hand. Mixture may take a further 10% extra water.
- Cover and ferment the dough for 2 hours.
- Tip out the dough on to a floured table.
- Pat out gently and fold into 3.
- Cover again and place in a cool area at 9 - 11°C for 2 hours.
- Roll out into an oblong and put the chilled Danish butter on 2/3 of the surface of the dough.
- Fold into 3 and chill for 30 minutes.
- Roll out into an oblong and fold into 3.
- Chill for 15 minutes.
- Repeat this again
- Roll out the dough and cut into strips, to suit the size of your pre-prepared tins. The dough should take about ¼ of the tin capacity.
- Prove until the dough reaches ½ of the tin size.
- Egg wash with care and bake. Bake at the higher temp to get lift from the lamination, and then reduce to avoid burning.

Rouen

It would appear that all roads lead to Rouen, or that was the view of the Romans in Gaulle. The early site of the city was a fording place for the river Seine. The Romans understood its importance and it was garrisoned on both sides of the river. Rouen is the capital of the lower Normandy region and is at the heart of the transport hub; river, road and rail links all converge at Rouen.

Artisan baking is still alive and kicking in the city but has suffered at the hands of the supermarket. The problem in the city is parking and getting to the smaller bakeries in the old town. Supermarkets provide easy access to the groceries and most large stores will have a working bakery on site. The in-store bakeries provide a good range of breads that are part baked or made on short fermentation processes. They look good and smell nice but lack the texture and flavour of real bread. This is the steady march of so called progress appearing in France. It is to be hoped that the French patriotic, stubborn love of good food will slow the loss of Bon Pain.

In culinary terms, Normand will usually infer an inclusion of apples or apple products. The local specialist bread is made with water and cider and is called *le pain Normand au cidre*, a rustic bread with white, wholemeal and rye flour in the recipe.

Ancient buildings

Pain la brie Normand

Cider apples

Pain la Brie Normand de Rouen

Ingredients

450g	Strong white bread flour*
135g	Water (27°C)
135g	Levain natural
7g	Yeast fresh
7g	Salt
25g	Butter

Total 759g

This bread can also be made with wholemeal, rye, or a blend.

Mixing Method

- Mix the flour and water together on slow speed for 3 minutes or by hand.
- Leave for 15 minutes.
- Add the levain natural and yeast.
- Mix for 5 minutes on slow speed, or by hand
- Add salt and butter mix for a further 6 minutes on 2nd or medium speed, by hand 12 minutes.
- Scale and mould roughly into balls.
- Rest for 15 minutes.
- Mould and shape into rugby balls.
- Prove for 2 hours.
- Cut and bake.

Dough temp:	25°C
Mixing water temp:	_____°C
1st speed mix time:	3 mins + 5 mins
2nd speed mix time:	6 mins (or 12 mins by hand)
1st fermentation time:	1 hour
Conditions:	Warm and covered
De-gas/knock back:	40 mins
Scale at:	375g
Yield:	2
Resting period:	15 mins
Tray tin type and size:	38 x 26cm
Warm/prepare:	Lightly greased
Shape and form dough:	Into rugby ball shapes
Prove at:	20°C for 2 hours
Pre-baking finish:	Just prior to baking cut dough length ways about 5 times
Oven temperature:	240°C (fan 230°C)
Baking time:	30 - 35 mins
Post baking finish:	Brush with melted butter immediately from oven

Approximate production time: 2 hours 30 mins
Product life: 2 - 3 days

Abbeville

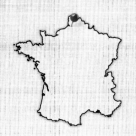

Abbeville, pronounced *Abveel*, is a remarkable place. It appears that the whole area should ooze history, but Abbeville the town has little to offer, apart from lots of bridges. Ancient Abbeville was an island in the Somme estuary when some bright spark established it as a refuge from the Norsemen, but seeing as they got around in long ships, perhaps it wasn't a very safe place to be.

The locality boasts the forest of Crécy, where Philippe VI and Edward III did battle. Philippe had heavily armoured Knights but Edward had a toughened band of English, Welsh and Scots infantry, supported by English and Welsh archers. Chivalry went out of the window that day, as the British commoners slaughtered the French nobility in the mud.

The French infantry found out far too late that the British could launch five arrows a minute at their mounted knights, while the French archers who used the crossbow could only reply with two arrows a minute. The law in England made young men and boys practice with longbow every Sunday, a law only repealed by the Betting and Gaming Act of 1960. They shot at targets on village greens and took the wood for their bows from yew trees grown in churchyards. This paid dividends on the battle field at Crecy, when their speed and accuracy helped to win the battle. Abbeville was also the site of battles in World War 1 and was extensively damaged by bombing in World War 2, which goes some way to explaining its relative lack of interesting landmarks today.

I would like to think that Bishop Honoré might have spent the night here on his way back to Amiens and home. I love open air markets in France and the one at Abbeville had two bread stalls. One appeared to favour breads with all manner of additions to the dough, breads with olives, cheese, smoked ham and my favourite; onion. As usual, I could not resist buying one of each of the bread types on sale.

Windmill

Market stall at Abbeville

Ducks on the canal at Abbeville

Pain a' l'Oignon au Lard (Onion & Bacon)

Ingredients

250g	White bread flour
250g	Levain natural
2g	Yeast fresh
6g	Salt*
155g	Water
65g	Diced fried bacon (lardons)
65g	Fried onions

Total 793g

Soften in a little hot water.

Dough temp:	21°C
Mixing water temp:	_____°C
1st speed mix time:	17 mins
1st fermentation time:	2 hours
Conditions:	Warm and covered
De-gas/knock back:	After 1 hour, then after 2 hrs
Scale at:	390g
Yield:	2
Resting period:	10 mins
Tray tin type and size:	38 x 26cm
Warm/prepare:	Lightly greased
Shape and form dough:	Into ovals
Prove at:	25°C for 90 mins
Pre-baking finish:	Cut along the length of the oval, place thick raw onion rings on the surface as decoration
Oven temperature:	220°C (fan 200°C)
Baking time:	30 - 35 mins
Conditions:	With added water in a tray
Post baking finish:	Glaze with a little bacon fat on exiting the oven

Approximate production time: 4 hours
Product life: 2 days

Mixing Method

- Place the flour, water, yeast and levain in a bowl.
- Mix for 10 minutes slow or by hand.
- Add the softened salt.
- Mix for a further 7 minutes on slow or by hand.
- Rest for 5 minutes.
- Turn out onto a chopping board.
- Cut the dough into cubes.
- Sprinkle the cooled bacon bits and the drained onions onto to the dough.
- Fold the dough and incorporate the bacon and onions.
- Place in a bowl covered for 2 hours
- De-gas after 1 hour.
- After 2 hours de-gas and scale at 390g.
- Shape into bâtards, length to suit your tray size.
- Rest for 5 minutes.
- Decorate with thick onion rings.

Baie de Somme

Located on the Picardy coast, is the bay of the Somme, which is now famous for its wildlife. Here wheat grows close to the fringe of the salt flats and has its own distinctive flavour. Local artisan bakers make bread called *pain Avocette* which is not available in the UK but worth looking out for if you are in the area.

The poppy, war and the Somme are for most Brits linked together by the Armistice parades and Remembrance Sunday. The poppy flourishes on freshly broken ground and there was plenty of that in 1916. The poppy still grows by the road sides and in the wheat fields of the Somme valley. Thankfully, the sounds and scars of war are now only a memory.

Locally the Baie de Somme railway steams up to Saint-Valery-sur-Somme. The train tows carriages that are more than 80 years old and on trains like these, young men where taken to the front line in 1916. The Somme is a happy place now with school tours and educational field trips, about the 1st World War, "Lest we forget".

My choice of bread is *pain Berche*, this is made from toasted poppy seeds. Berche is shaped like a rugby ball with a thin plait of dough along its length; this is then decorated with more poppy seeds and baked.

Thiepval Memorial

Ship wreck

Poppy field

Berche (Poppy Seed Bread)

Ingredients

500g	Bread flour
320g	Water (38°C)
7g	Salt
8g	Yeast fresh
150g	Pre-ferment dough
60g	Poppy seeds (lightly toasted)
20g	Poppy seeds for dressing (not toasted)

Total 1.65kg

Dough temp:	24°C
Mixing water temp:	_____°C
1st speed mix time:	10 mins
2nd speed mix time:	7 mins (or 10 mins by hand)
1st fermentation time:	90 mins
Conditions:	Ambient and covered
De-gas/knock back:	45 mins
Scale at:	480g and 20g
Yield:	2 plus 4 rolls
Resting period:	15 mins
Tray tin type and size:	38 x 26cm
Warm/prepare:	Lightly greased
Shape and form dough:	Oval with a crease for the plait to sit in
Prove at:	28°C for 1 hour
Pre-baking finish:	Poppy seeds along the sides of the loaf
Oven temperature:	230°C (fan 220°C)
Baking time:	25 - 30 mins
Conditions:	With humidity for first 15 mins
Post baking finish:	Spray lightly with cold water on exit from the oven

Approximate production time: 3 hours
Product life: 1 - 2 days

Mixing Method

- Place the flour and salt in a mixing bowl.
- Dissolve the fresh yeast in the tepid water and add to the flour.
- Mix for 10 minutes on slow or by hand.
- Add the pre-fermented dough and the toasted poppy seeds.
- Mix for a further 7 minutes on medium speed or by hand 10 minutes.
- Cover and ferment for 90 minutes.
- De-gas after 45 minutes.
- After 90 minutes, scale the dough at 480g, mould round, also scale dough at 20g x 4 and mould round.
- Rest for 15 minutes.
- Mould again into rugby ball shapes.
- Roll out the 20g balls into spaghettis, two and half times the length of the loaf.
- Make a 2 strand plait for each loaf
- Form a crease in the centre of the loaf.
- Moisten and apply the plait loosely to the loaf, firm in position.
- Spray with water, apply poppy seeds to the sides of the loaf.
- Fully prove, then bake.

Section Three

Ancient castle

Mosaic pilgrim

Pain Flame

Pave Graines

Glossary of Terms (Lexique Professionnal)

English	Français	English	Français
Bread Making	**Les Etapes de la Panification**	**Ingredients**	**Les Ingredients**
Baking	la caisson	Additives	l'additif
Bread cutting	la coupe	Bakery yeast	la levure de boulangerie
First fermentation	le pointage		
Kneading	le pétrissage	Butter	le beurre
Round shaping	le boulage	Egg	l'oeuf
Second fermentation	l'apprêt	Fat	la margarine
Shaping	le façonnage	Flour	la farine
The baker	le boulanger	Milk	le lait
The bakery	le fournil	Rye flour	la farine de seigle
The crumb	la mie	Salt	le sel
The crust	la croûte	Sour dough	le levain
The dough	la pâte	Strong flour	la farine de force
The oven	le four	Sugar	le sucre
The steam	la buée	Water	l'eau
The strength	la force	Wheat flour	la farine de blé
To put in the oven (enfourner)	l'enfournement	Whole meal flour	la farine complét
To take out of the oven (défourner)	le défournement		
Waiting/resting time	la détente		
Weighting	le pesage		

The legal requirement for bread to be described as "rye bread" requires a minimum of 65% rye flour with 35% wheat flour.

Lower amounts of rye flour e.g. 50% rye and 50% wheat is termed *méteil*. Bread made from this blend is termed as *pain de méteil*.

English	Français
Bread made with 85% white bread flour and 15% rye flour	pain de campagne
Made with 75% white bread flour and 25% rye flour	pain paysan
A less enriched version of brioche, often toasted and served with pâté & foie gras.	pain brioché
Bread cut to represent ears of wheat	pain épi
Large loaf often rectangular with rounded corners	miche
Cobble stones, irregular shapes of bread produced by cutting the dough into pieces	pavé
French traditional breads	le pain classique
Decorated breads	les pain décorés
Speciality breads	les pain speciaux
Viennese baking	les viennoiseries

Top Tips for New Home Bakers

Recipe Conversion

If you need to convert an older recipe from pounds and ounces, use 30g for 1 ounce to make your calculations. The correct 28g to 1 oz will give you lots of odd numbers to work with. Water levels in recipes will only serve as a guide; the amount of water a given flour will absorb, will depend on some or all of the following.

The method of milling used by the miller, the protein/gluten content of the flour, the type of flour, white, brown if it's a rye or a wheat and rye mixture. If there are other ingredients present like milk solids and seeds and even the mixing method chosen can play a part.

Extra bran equals extra water. French bread is made with the maximum amount of water the flour will carry. This amount can vary from batch to batch of flour. In French bread 65% water is normal and many will have more. However, if it looks too wet or too dry go with your instinct and amend the mixture, but not necessarily the recipe, just make a note for next time.

Is it Baked?

You have four senses to help you:

Smell
Baked bread has its own smell, brought about by the caramelised sugars on the bread surface.

Sight
You can see if it is about right to take out of the oven, or if the oven is too hot by the colour. The colour can be misleading with wholemeal bread as it goes to the oven brown.

Touch
You can assess the degree of baking by touch (do it quickly to avoid burns)

Hearing
A fully baked loaf will have a hollow sound if you tap the base. If you bake the same sized loaves at a constant temperature baking times should be fairly predictable. Remember to ventilate your room, when you load your oven. Open the oven door and step back as you do it, to avoid a red face.

- Sleeves up for mixing and down for oven work.
- Clean as you go, no knives in the sink and no wet oven cloths, please.
- Pastry and cake flour should not be used for bread making only for flour decoration.

"The Baker" and his wife

French Breads to Serve with Classic Meals

Perhaps you are planning to cook a special meal to recreate a holiday moment or a dinner party for friends. This guide shows just some of the many ways the French will eat bread with their meals.

Multi Seed Breads	Enhance the flavour of chicken and thinly sliced cooked meats.
Pain au Lait	Is served to hungry children with hot chocolate in the afternoon.
Pain au Son (Bran Bread)	Is eaten with cheeses, green salad and terrine.
Pain Auvergne	Made with blue cheese goes well with salad vegetables.
Pain Brioche	Sliced and toasted and served with a smooth pâté or foie gras.
Pain Château Brissac	Fruited bread complements the flavour of game meats.
Pain Château Pimpean	To eat with cold meats and pickles.
Pain Complet	Sits well on a plate with red and white roasted meats.
Pain le Brie Normand	Sliced, toasted, buttered with a smoked oyster on top.
Pain Muesli	Is a natural for breakfast.
Pain Six Ceriales	Good for breakfast, but is often served with roasted pork and game.
Paysan and Campagne	Are often eaten with cheese, fish, crudités, terrine and pâté.
Rye Bread	Will complement the stronger flavours of blue cheese and sea food.
Rye with Raisin	Can be served at breakfast or with afternoon tea.
White Bread	Can be eaten with any meal.

In my opinion you are the best judge of which bread to choose and use for that special occasion.

French Flour Classification System

If you purchase a French book of bread recipes, it may be useful to be able to convert them for use in the United Kingdom. The French system uses numbers rather than names, as we do in the UK. Some French flours have similar UK equivalents, but there are many that do not.

The French system will have a type number, e.g. T55. Where possible I will give nearest UK flour adjacent to the French flour.

Code	Description	Nearest UK equivalent
T45.	Used for pain gruau, brioche and croissants etc	Extra strong white bread flour
T55.	Used for baguettes	Strong white bread flour
T65.	General purpose bread flour for country breads	Strong off white bread flour
T80.	Suitable for traditional breads	Strong semi-white bread flour
T110.	Pain paysan	Strong brown bread flour
T150.	Pain complet	Strong (nearly) wholemeal bread flour

Rye flours

Code	Description	Nearest UK equivalent
T85.	Used in pain campagne	Light rye flour
T130.	Used in pain paysan and meteil	Medium rye flour
T170.	Used for black rye breads	Dark rye flour

Ideas for Using Leftover Bread

- White bread crumbs in treacle tarts
- White bread slices in bread and butter pudding
- A whole, stale round loaf can have the top sliced off and the crumbs removed. This can then be filled with little snacks or sandwiches and put on the table.
- French toast - Bread soaked in seasoned egg and milk then fried in butter, a children's favourite.
- Bread crumbs can be used to coat pork, chicken and fish. Then deep fry.
- Pain brioche toasted and topped with smoked oysters
- Brioche makes a luxury bread and butter pudding

- Baguettes cut length ways (with care) can be smeared with olive oil, tomato purée, basil, pesto and topped with cheese, for a pizza snack.
- Baguettes can be run under the tap and toasted under a pre-heated grill; this would be alright for instant hot bread with jam and coffee.
- Welsh rabbit (rarebit)
- Toasted sandwiches
- Brochette with any topping you like
- Sides of a summer pudding
- Cheese toast rafts, to float on French onion soup
- Mixed with lard and hung in the garden for the birds

Pâté and toast

Milling

For any grain to be of maximum food value to humans, it must first be crushed and opened. In order to do this pots and sticks were used, thumping the grain and splitting it open. This can still be seen in rural Africa. Later the saddle stone provided the shearing action to tear apart the grain casing.

Milling by hand can be seen in Egyptian tomb wall paintings and must have been back breaking work. Crushed grains have been found in beakers buried as grave goods, these to be taken into the after life, a snack on reaching your final destination. The Romans used the milling process. Rome had its millers and bakers to supply the growing population of the city. Scaled down mill stones could be transported by pack animals for the army. Highly portable, these stones could be producing flour for the legion as soon as their chosen site was secured.

This type of milling was designed so that the top stones moved and the base stone was stationary. As the top stone turns it crushes and breaks the grain reducing it to coarse flour called meal. Because the whole of the grain is used it is called wholemeal. This is then sieved and the large pieces are returned to the mill stone for further treatment (see "Folklore" for Rule of Thumb) Sieved flour was fairly course stuff, the nobility would have finer flour and the King and Queen had flour passed through silk.

Windmills

In upland areas water was not always available to the miller. Windmills would be the solution for power. The first windmills were a fixed construction with the mill's sail built on the wind side of the construction. Wind does not always blow from the same direction, so the next development was to build the top section on a movable housing. The sails could then be directed into the wind by pushing a long tiller around so the sails were pointing into the wind.

Grain grinding wheel

As populations grew, the demand for milled flour increased and mill stones needed to be made larger. Size created its own problems, the larger mill stone could no longer be powered by humans. Large animals, bullocks, donkeys and horses provided the power. The animals walked in a circle turning the mill stone as they moved along.

Watermills

These were first recorded in England in A.D. 1086, the great census, often known as the Doomsday Book. Watermills were built at the lower ends of valleys in order to harvest the flow of river water. Most water courses however did not have the flow/force to continuously serve the mill. The solution was to dig out a route for the water and create a dam just prior to the mill wheel. Man-made water courses were known as *leets*. I suspect the technology was taken from the systems and cisterns used by monastic builders. In fact there was an order of monks called Cistercians who were famous for their water management techniques.

If the mill buildings could be built lower than the mills dam, the water could be directed to fall on the far side of the wheel. This was called an over shot system, because the weight of the water fell onto the wheel and it generated the most power possible to the mill wheel. The water flow was controlled by a sluice gate; if this was closed water would be diverted back to the river. Mills that did not have the advantage of a raised water source would use the under shot system. The water flow would pass under the wheel, the wheel was constructed with broad wooden paddles in order to maximise contact with the water flow. Not the most efficient system but the one adopted by mills located in flatter parts of France.

Windmills (*Le Moulin à Vent*) are often adopted by towns and village and restored, being put back to work turning out flour for *pain complet*. Later there was steam and roller milling. Flour was milled and separated into starch, bran and germ. This gave the miller the ability to produce white flour with ease. Blends of rye and wheat, barley and seeds could be produced with interesting combinations.

Then came the Industrial Revolution, with steam power, but that's another story...

Watermill at Bayeux

The Simple Physics and Chemistry of Baking

Bread dough once placed in the oven will gradually increase in temperature. As the dough temperature increases, there will be heightened yeast activity. Carbon dioxide gas rapidly produced will fill the gas pockets within the dough. Steam also being produced will contribute to the further expansion of the loaf.

Heat will gelatinize the starch and coagulate the gluten (wheat protein). This coagulation and gelatinization will give the loaf its internal structure. By now yeast and the enzymes will have been killed off by the high internal temperature. The small amount of ethyl alcohol will have evaporated as the loaf temperature increases.

The outer surface of the dough (crust) will have started to take colour, this due to the natural sugar maltose in the flour caramelising, adding extra flavour to the dough.

Brown, wholemeal and rye breads can be a bit misleading to the new baker. Already brown in colour, you can be fooled into thinking the loaf is baked.

Baking bread on tiles in a domestic oven

Colour, time, feel and the hollow sound, all of these must be fully employed when assessing a baked loaf. Baking times are a guide but there is no substitute for experience. Milk and extra added sugar can cause your loaves, for example brioche, to burn, so I advise lowering the temperature (see recipe).

The baked loaf will smell baked (sorry but a fully baked loaf has its own smell). It will feel right, it should not be too soft; squeeze and it will have some spring. Colour is also an indication, but not so much for wholemeal bread and most bread will sound hollow if the base of the loaf is tapped.

Cautionary Note on Crust Colour:
Research carried out on wheat and potato starch indicate that higher temperatures in baking and frying produces a material called Acrylamide. This is thought to be associated with low birth weights in pregnant women and heightens the risk of cancer in general. So keep the toast on the light side and do not over bake your bread, this would appear to be sound advice and the healthy option.

Part Baking
It is possible to bake bread and rolls for a dinner party in advance by freezing. Remove them from the oven when just a little brown, cool and freeze. Defrost an hour before the meal, spray with a little water and place in a pre-heated oven, 230°C (fan 220°C) for about five minutes or until lightly brown. Wonderful served with French onion soup.

Folklore and Myth

Upper Crust

An old reference to the rich folk at the big house. Bread baked in wood fired ovens would scorch and burn on the bottom. If you were gentry the top section was cut off, the lower part of the loaf would also be cut off, making you a cut above some one else. The poor got the remaining burnt base, perhaps being told to eat it! "It will make your hair curl".

To use your Loaf

Meaning to think before you act. It is thought that soldiers put their loaves on their bayonets and raised them above the earth parapet to check for the presence of sharp shooters.

Deadly Bread

A group of Jews who had survived the Nazi death camps set out to avenge their lost friends. Plan A being to poison the water supply of several big cities. This failed as they could not get sufficient quantities of poison to make the water sufficiently dangerous.

Plan B was to poison the bread rations of a camp full of captured SS camp guards. One of the group joined the bakers in the camp on night shift. After work he hid away and, prior to the bread being issued, he painted the bread tops with a poisonous glaze. The bread dried, cooled and was issued to the Nazi guards. They soon became ill, and, as the war was over, fleets of American ambulances ferried the poisoned Germans to the now virtually empty hospitals. There they were tended to and, as I understand, no one died.

Bread and Circuses

In ancient Rome citizens had a flour allowance. This along with entertainment at the circus Maximus was intended to keep the population happy, hence the expression, bread and circuses.

Never on a Sunday

Bread baking in France was the only occupation given Church approval to work on Sundays. Sadly the world turns and things have changed.

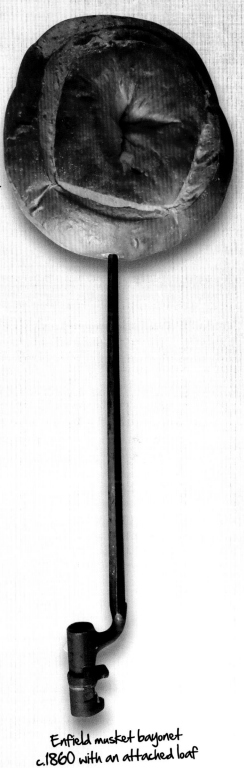

Enfield musket bayonet c.1860 with an attached loaf

137

The Body of Christ

Bread has, through Christian tradition, been a very important item. Communion wafers were made by bakers and bread symbolised the body of Christ and the Staff of Life. In Malta it was considered bad luck to drop bread on the ground. People finding it on the ground would place it on a wall or off the ground.

Table Manners

It is still considered bad etiquette by some to cut a bread roll with a knife at dinner, better to break bread with family and friends.

Happy Accident

Long before the discovery of penicillin, mouldy bread with penicillin on was used to draw the infection out of wounds.

Fuel Poverty

The fuel wealth of a country can often be judged by the thickness of its bread. Very thin breads often originate from areas with few trees and little fuel. Lots of wood and coal will equate with larger units of bread.

Bread and Tradition

Bread and salt is a traditional greeting in much of Russia and Eastern Europe.

Special and Festival Breads

Most of Europe, including France, has festival bread. In Holland, on reaching the age of retirement, it is customary to produce large sweet bread decorated in the shape of a woman, "*Sarah*" and for the man "*Abraham*".

Christmas Bread

Germany has Christmas night enriched bread called *Weihnach Stollen*. This is exported across the miles to Germanic peoples all over the world.

Kings Cake

France has *Gateau des Rois*, a brioche with an attached gold paper crown. Inside the bread is placed a santon (a very small glazed figurine) and the person who discovers it in their tranche is King or Queen for the day. The family members are obliged to fetch and carry for them all day. Because of the santons, take care with your National Health Service crown!

Hieroglyphs

The Egyptians had a symbol for bread: their love of refined flour which often had bits of grit in it maybe from the mill stones. It may have been the cause of the dreadful tooth decay found in the mummies that have been exhumed and examined.

Dry Cleaning

Many years ago men and women took a bath twice a year. The custom amongst the rich was to wear wigs. Men shaved their heads to reduce the problem of lice, nits and fleas. Wigs for the wealthy men were generally made from wool and these made fine houses for any infestation. It was not possible to put the wigs in a boil wash as they would shrink and distort.

The answer to the problem was to cut the top off a large loaf, scoop out the crumb and place the wig inside putting the top back on. The whole loaf with the wig inside was put in the oven. The heat killed the bugs and served to fluff up the wig. It was early dry cleaning and another way to use your loaf.

Barm Pot

The barm pot was a pre-industrial revolution device. Wild yeast from plums placed in an earthenware pot, fed with rye flour and honey and kept warm was your yeast source. This is our version of *le levain naturel* nearly lost in time. Most of this mixture was used on baking days. Topped up and fed with flour, honey and water the barm would be ready for the next bake in a day or two. Hence barm cakes from the barm pot. In Lancashire you are a barm pot, which is a mild insult. Barmy is a reference to the frothing of the pot and the discredited association with the mentally ill.

Mothers, whose daughters left the family home, gave them a hazel twig dipped several times in the barm pot and dried to take with them. A pot of water, flour, honey and the hazel twig would seed another barm pot, if the plums could not be obtained or were out of season.

Pain Complet

The French bread *pain complet*, means just what it says, all of the wheat including the beard, (hairy bits) that you see on French wheat and barley. All of the wheat grain goes into the flour blend; this then is the French term "complete".

The Rule of Thumb

This is a miller's and baker's term, rubbing flour between the fingers and thumb to assess the quantity of the flour e.g, the amount of coarse particles present.

Beer

This was a vital source of uncontaminated liquid, all the bacteria being killed by boiling, thus giving medieval men and women a safe drink, as water was often suspect. As the population increased, water supplies were often found to be polluted.

Small Beer

The term small beer was low alcohol beer for children.

Miller, Brewer and Baker

The village traders had a symbiotic relationship. The miller milled the wheat and often malted the barley. The flour would be baked into bread with addition of yeast remaining after the brewing process. The brewer got his natural sugar from the malted barley and re-used some of his yeast to create more beer.

The Miller

Would no doubt have taken bread and ale as part of his payment.

Brown Bread

Cockney rhyming slang has brown bread... For dead!

This is an ancient grain store, fully ventilated and built with legs to deter vermin. Note the added ring round the legs to prevent the rats climbing up

Ergotisme ("The Devil's Kiss")

A warning from history that may return

In the mid 1600s, England appeared to have suffered a number of poor summers. It rained through to the late summer harvest periods. With no way to dry the stoops, the rye harvest would have been taken from the fields damp. Under such conditions the ergot, a mould that grows on rye grains in the fields, would have grown further in the tythe barns. The tythe system was a form of taxation, equal to one tenth of the crop. The church and nobility levied this tax on the peasants who worked their land.

Bread contaminated with ergot would give the victim hallucinations, a sort of LSD trip. To others, the blood supply was reduced and cut off their extremities, resulting in gangrenous limbs, madness and death. In some poor souls deformities of legs and arms were recorded. After the first contaminated bread consumed, people became more sensitive to the ergot not less. Smaller and smaller amounts of contamination brought about increased reaction in the individuals affected.

There are some disturbing images of people who may have suffered this fate, painted by Pieter Bruegel de Ounde circa 1568. One of those canvases is to be found in the Lourve, Paris. France had it's fair share of Ergotisme with possible outbreaks recorded in Orleans as early as 1089 and again in 1109. The greatest number of outbreaks is recorded between the years 1630 – 1700. They seem to have had some of the worst reported outbreaks over Europe and the colonies. There is a clear link between poor weather conditions and Ergotisme. Now farmers have grain driers so rye and wheat is checked for moisture content prior to storage. There were recorded incidents in France as late as 1855 and then it seems the problem may have been resolved.

It was in the 1600s that the incidents of women being accused of witchcraft increased. The clergy were unable to help as people affected by the LSD style trip threw themselves off the top of the church towers. The devil in full pursuit drove others to drown themselves, as villagers looked on in horror. It was then that the infamous witch trials started. People, who had eaten infected bread, saw devils and thought they had been cursed. The solution, find a woman with a cat and perhaps a pet raven.

She would be denounced and tried, ducking her on the ducking stool in the river. If she drowned then she was innocent and if she did not drown she was a witch. Burning at the stake came next and if the problem persisted, find a neighbour they disliked and accuse her. A "Witch Finder General" was appointed and a lot of innocent women were put to death. Similar problems were experienced in Europe and the Americas. They even made a film about Salem and Beverly, New England.

In the space of twenty years the United Kingdom stopped eating rye as their staple food. They appeared to experiment with beans, oats and peas and finally got to wheat without any scientific knowledge to formally identify what caused the dreadful illness that afflicted so many. Rye as a name is all around, Ryedale and a pocketful of rye are clues to our past.

So England lost the taste for rye and with access to the Canadian wheat fields, bakers in England all stopped making rye bread. In France, as in the rest of Europe, rye still plays a big part in bread making. As you move to the east of Europe, Germany, Poland and Russia, grow and consume more in a week than we eat in a year.

Remember, the Ergot has not gone away. A friend saw it and photographed it growing on a rye crop in Yorkshire, England. As we import more varied seeds and grains for bread making an awareness of the problems of the past is important to remember. It could be closer than we think!

The Devil's Kiss

Some Ingredients and Equipment Suppliers

Russum - www.russums.co.uk
Catering, clothing and equipment

www.olive-design.co.uk
Mini peel and bread display boards.

www.joshuathomascarpentry.com
Mini peels can also be obtained from here.

Tiles to bake on can be obtained from your local DIY store. Choose two thick unglazed red quarry tiles, (although tiles with a corner missing can be purchased at a discount price and work just as well as the perfect ones).

Pizza stones can also be baked on with excellent results, but cost more than tiles.

Flour - www.dovefarm-organic.co.uk
Rye and wholemeal flours.

Flour - www.shipton-mill.com
Spelt and chestnut flour.

French flour - www.fwpmatthews.co.uk

Yeast fresh
Check out the chill section of a big supermarket. Ask the staff as it can be hard to locate in big stores.

Some Thoughts on Buying Ingredients

If you can find some friends and family to form a buying Co-op you will get quality ingredients at a lower price. If you bake regularly you and your friends can seek out a bakery sundries supplier.

Divide large bags between your groups. Yeast is sold by 1kg blocks, again divided between a group it will get used and also it will freeze, when it comes out of the freezer use it as a poolish.

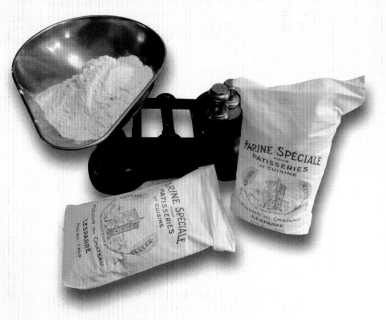

Bibliography

Les Pains Français   Philippe Roussel and Hubert Chiron

The Taste of Bread   Raymond Calvel - Translated by Ronald L. Wirtz
                                                     and James J. MacGuire

Brood Doet Leven   Claude Machevel & Renaud Zeebroek

The Modern Baker, Confection   John Kirkland
and Caterer Volume IV

Michelin Tourist Guide of France

And Finally...

Having followed the route that Bishop Honoré might have taken, I thought it might be appropriate to seek an opinion from a real live bishop. I wrote to the Archbishop of Westminster; Cardinal Vincent Nichols and the Archbishop of York; John Sentamu. In truth, I hold both of these men in high regard.

They are incredibly busy people, but both replied to my letters. The Archbishop of York wrote that "It was a wonderful idea", while the Cardinal wrote "I was fascinated to read about St Honoré and intrigued by the project".

I will be sending them both a copy of this book. It is nice to know that our religious leaders can still take a moment to reply to me.

Credits

Thanks go to:

Patrick Bastiani (France)
Chris Tomson (UK)
Richard North (UK)
Chris Ogden Productions for the DVD (UK)
Jamie Mann Graphic Design (UK)

For the photographic contributions to my book.

Lynn Hinchliff
Gemma Mann
Proof reading.

Matthew and Ruth North
For their support.

Brian Smailes
Consultant.

Pamela Smailes
Editing.

Please Note

The photographs that appear in my book are not taken by professionals. The wonderful photographs we see in books are often "stage managed" with products made over and over until the perfect image is achieved.

The photographs taken are hand held shots taken with a Sony Exmor. They are intended to look amateur because they are! Pictures are of bread and doughs as they were being made, no special lighting, just honest photo snaps. Photographs of people and places are equally honest, just as I saw them at the time.

Post Script

I have often mused about the many people and places that have links to my book. On a recent follow-up visit to France we were robbed of our passports. The officials at the campsites of Bayeux and Château Renault were understanding and helpful. The Gendarmerie National were also pleasant, efficient and provided all the legal paperwork.

To replace a stolen passport involves a visit to the British embassy in Paris, who were also efficient and friendly. The address of the embassy? Yes, you guessed it - Rue St Honoré!

So the book is finished and the circle is complete. It started in Paris at the Bakery School and ends at the embassy in Paris, on both occasions with St Honoré...

Notes